PICTURE POSTERS

YVETTE GUILBERT. FACSIMILE OF SKETCH BY TOULOUSE-
LAUTREC FOR AN UNPUBLISHED POSTER.

PICTURE POSTERS

By CHARLES HIATT

EP PUBLISHING LIMITED
1976

Republished 1976 by
EP Publishing Limited
East Ardsley, Wakefield
West Yorkshire, England

First published 1895 by
George Bell and Sons, London

ISBN 0 7158 1150 9

British Library Cataloguing in Publication Data

HIATT, Charles
  Picture posters.
  Index.
  ISBN 0-7158-1150-9
  1. Ti
  DC. 769' .5
  LC. NC 1810
  LCSH. Posters – History

Please address all enquiries to EP Publishing Limited
(address as above)

Printed in Great Britain by
REDWOOD BURN LIMITED
Trowbridge & Esher

CONTENTS.

INDEX OF ILLUSTRATIONS.

INDEX OF ILLUSTRATIONS.   xiii

PREFACE.

IN the present volume an attempt has been made briefly to trace the history of the picture poster from the earliest times, and to comment upon and reproduce some of the most noteworthy examples in various countries. The English and American placards have received special attention, while the best examples of the French school have not been overlooked. With very few exceptions, only posters signed, or acknowledged, by the artists producing them, are included among the illustrations. The whole subject is treated from the point of view rather of art than of commerce. While it is believed that this book is the first which deals in English with the Pictorial Poster, the author desires to recognize his indebtedness to M. Maindron's work, and to the catalogues of M. Sagot and Mr. Bella. The last-named has rendered material aid by lending, for the purpose of reproduction, not a few examples contained in his collection.

To name the artists and owners of valuable copyrights who have laid the author under obligations would, however carefully compiled, almost certainly contain serious *omissions. It is hoped, therefore, that those whose names would figure in such a list will acquit him of intentional discourtesy or ingratitude. Special thanks are due to Mr. Gleeson White for his editorial work in connection with this volume; indeed, whatever merits it may possess are due, in no small degree, to his care and assiduity. Although personally unknown to the writer, Mr. Spielmann has been so good as to assist materially in the matter of illustration. To the kindness of M. Henri de Toulouse-Lautrec is owing the frontispiece in the shape of a hitherto unpublished study for a poster; while the reproduction of a sketch for the "Phit-Eesi" placard was courteously consented to by Mr. Dudley Hardy, and Messrs. Waterlow who printed the poster itself. The cover has been specially drawn by Mr. Charles Ffoulkes, to whom the writer desires to express his sincere thanks. The Artistic Supply Company (Limited) have been so good as to consent to the reproduction of unpublished copyright designs by Messrs. Bernard Partridge, Max Cowper, the Brothers Beggarstaff, Sydney Adamson, Kerr Lawson, A. R. Wilson, and Lewis Baumer. A design, representing Sir Henry Irving as "Don Quixote," is illustrated here owing to the kindness of Miss Ellen Terry, who owns the original.*

C<small>HARLES</small> H<small>IATT</small>.

October, 1895.

PICTURE POSTERS.

CHAPTER I.

THE STORY OF THE PICTORIAL POSTER.

It would be merely foolish to pretend that the pictorial poster, looked at from the point of view of art, is of the same importance as a portrait by Velasquez or an etching by Rembrandt. Its æsthetic qualities have of necessity to be subordinated to its commercial qualities ; the artist is the servant of the tradesman. His first business is not to achieve a decoration, but to call the attention of the man in the street to the merits of an article. He may be fantastic only in so far as his fantasy assists the advertisement ; he must ever keep before his eyes the narrow object of his effort. The closest limits are set to his invention ; it is not for him to do what he will, but rather to do what he must. Under such circumstances, it is, at the first blush, somewhat surprising that artists have condescended to the poster at all. The bounds of freedom in the cases of painting and of sculpture are, comparatively speaking, so wide that one is not unnaturally amazed that the artist of talent is willing to work within the strict limitations imposed on him in the production of a pictorial poster. And yet, after all, to the ingenious designer there is a certain fascination in the very strictness of these limits; the complexity of the problem allures him, and gives him the appetite for experiment. Moreover, if he believe that art is something more than a vague grace, a non-essential luxury, he is ever anxious to extend her domain, to make her empire universal. He believes it to be his mission to touch some ugly necessity, to inform it with art, and, in doing so, to adorn it. He is restless for new worlds to conquer, for fresh fields to occupy. His ideal is art everywhere, art in all. He would fain give style and grace even to the paraphernalia of commerce : the necessities of trade shall not be hideous if he can make them otherwise. And so it happens that he is willing, nay eager, to turn his attention to the poster, with the result that the hoarding becomes an interesting, even a charming, gallery of designs. What was one of the most hideous of human inventions is transformed into a delight to the eyes. Colour and interest are added to the street ; the gay and joyous take the place of the dull and ugly.

It follows, supposing that I have stated the case fairly, that it is not derogatory to the dignity, even of a very great artist, to apply his talent to the poster.

It is clear that the poster is one of the oldest and most obvious forms of advertisement. It is almost impossible to conceive a time in the history of man, once he had learned to express his thoughts in design or in writing, when the idea of the thing did not exist. It must have been an incident of the most crude and ancient of civilizations; even the cave-dweller in the dim and distant past must surely have possessed the essential idea of it. From the cave-dweller to the comparatively complex civilization of the ancient and greater Egypt is a far cry. That the mural inscription, which is obviously the germ of the poster, flourished exceedingly in the Land of the Pharaohs is matter of history. A papyrus is comprised in the collections of the Louvre, which may fairly be described as a poster. It is dated so early as 146 B.C., and deals at length with the escape of two slaves from the city of Alexandria, offering a reward to anybody who should discover their place of retreat. Still more interesting, though less ancient, is an inscription in Greek, discovered in the Temple at Jerusalem, in 1872, by M. Clermont-Gannerau. It was issued during the reign of Herod the Great, and forbids the entry, by foreigners, to certain parts of the Temple on pain of death.

Of the poster in Greece we know very little. Legal inscriptions were undoubtedly written on whitened walls, or on *axones*, the latter being wooden tablets painted white, and made to revolve slowly on an upright axis. In passing from Greece to Rome, we pass from somewhat fragmentary to comparatively exact information. The Roman notice-board was called an *album*, and it is a matter of dispute whether it was white with black letters, or of a dark colour with the text in white. Anybody who took away, destroyed, or mutilated an *album* was liable to an *actio albi corrupti*, and to heavy damages besides. It appears to have been invented in the first place, in order to give publicity to the annual edict of the Prætor; subsequently, however, the word *album* was used to signify any tablet on which a public announcement was inscribed. The ruins of Pompeii have furnished us with at least one interesting fragment of an *album*, on which are written notices of the most diverse kinds. Amongst them are the following:

FAMILIA . GLADIATORIA
VENATIO . ET . VELA .

and:

A. SVETTII . CERII .
AEDILIS . FAMILIA . GLADIATORIA . PUGNAVIT .
POMPEIS . PR . K. IVNIAS . VENATIO . ET . VELA .
ERUNT .

and again :

DEDICATIONE.
THERMARUM . MUNERIS .
ENAI . ALLEI . NIGIDII .
MAII . VENALIO . ATHELA .
SPARSIONES . VELA .
ERUNT . MAIO . PRINCIPI .
COLONIÆ . FELICITER .

As for the Roman bookseller, he was in the habit of placarding his shop with the titles of books just published, or about to be published. Take, for instance, the shop described by Martial in the lines :

"Contra Caesaris est forum taberna,
Scriptis postibus hinc et inde totis,
Omnes ut cito perlegas poetas.
Illinc me pete.

The actor has never been inclined to hide his light under a bushel. Advertisement has always been dear to him, and it is not surprising to find that the Roman actor made the most of the opportunity of the publicity offered to him by the *album*. Not content with having his name inscribed in gigantic letters, he went a step further, and anticipated the illustrated *affiche*. Just as Sarah Bernhardt employs the decorative skill of Grasset to depict her as Joan of Arc, so did the old Roman actor employ Callades, an artist mentioned very favourably by Pliny, to portray him in his favourite parts. Callades would seem to

have been the Chéret of his age : he was the
great artistic advertiser of ancient Rome,
just as Chéret is the great artistic advertiser
of modern Paris.

It is obvious, then, that the idea of the
illustrated poster existed among the Romans:
the difference between Callades and Chéret
is one of method rather than of vital prin-
ciple. And even the difference in method
is slight.

Of the poster in the time which immediately succeeded the fall of the Roman
Empire we have very little trustworthy information. It is possible that the Romans
introduced the *album* into Gaul and into
Britain, and that the sight of it became as
familiar to the inhabitants of Eboracum and
Uriconium as it was to the natives of Rome
and Pompeii. A French historian of distinction has stated that the *affiche* was employed by the earliest of the kings of France,
but this statement can hardly be said to be
borne out by facts. It is at least certain
that the signboard, which is a variation of the
pictorial poster, was employed in the early
part of the Middle Ages. The poster, unless
illustrated, would have been useless in a
community in which the art of writing was
held effeminate, in which the most illustrious
knight openly boasted of his inability to
sign his name. The principal means of advertisement at that time was the public crier.

As early as the twelfth century the criers of

France formed an organized body, " for," as
Mr. Sampson tells us in his *History of
Advertising*, " by a charter of Louis VII.
granted in the year 1141 to the inhabitants
of the province of Berry, the old custom of
the country was confirmed, according to
which there were to be only twelve criers, *criers*
five of whom should go about the taverns
crying with their usual cry, and carrying
with them samples of the wine they cried in
order that people might taste. For the first
time they blew the horn they were entitled to
a penny, and the same for every time after,
according to custom. . . . These wine-
criers are mentioned by John de Garlando,
a Norman writer, who was probably contemporary with William the Conqueror."
The wine-crier is frequently mentioned in
early French street-ballads. To instance
one of them :

> " Si crie l'on en plusors leurs
> Si bon vui fort a trente deux
> A seize, a douze, a six, a huiet."

In England also the crier was an early
institution, for we find one Edmund le
Criour mentioned in a document dated 1299.
Even when the crier was the pre-eminent
advertiser, the poster, or at least the hand-
bill, had its place. At first the bills were
written, but almost as soon as Caxton introduced the newly-discovered art of printing
they were produced by that method. Per-

haps the earliest English poster is that by which Caxton, about the year 1480, announced the " Pyes of Salisbury Use," at the Red Pole in the Almonry at Westminster. The size of this broadside is five inches by seven, and the text runs as follows :

" If it please any man spirituel or temporel to bye our pyes of two or thre comemoracio's of Salisburi use, emprunted after the form of this prese't lettre, which ben wel and truly correct, late hym come to Westmonster, into the almonestrye at the reed pole ane he shall have them good and chepe.
" Supplico stet cedula."

The "pyes" in question, it may be noted, were a series of diocesan rules.

It is in the sixteenth century that we meet with the poster properly so called. For example, we have a royal proclamation of François I relating to the police of the city of Paris, which runs : " Nous voulons que ces présentes ordonnances soient publiées tous les moys de l'an, par tous les quarrefours de' cette ville de Paris et faux bourgs d'icelle, à son de trompe et cry public. Et néantmoins qu'elles soient attachées a un tableau, escriptes en parchemain et en grosse lettre, en tous les seize quartiers de ladite ville de Paris es esdictz faux bourgs, et lieux les plus éminents et apparens d'iceulx, afin qu'elles soient cognues et entendues parfun chacun. Et qu'il ne soit loysible oster les dictz tableaux, sur peine de punition corporelle, dont les dictz commissaires auront la charge chacun en son quartier."

The words "attachées a un tableau, escriptes en parchemain et en grosse lettre" leave no doubt that the poster as we now know it was a usual method of advertisement in the reign of François Ier. The *affiche* soon after received the attention of the French legislature, for the production and exhibition of posters of certain kinds in France, was expressly forbidden by "un arrêt du Parlement" dated the 7th of February, 1652. To publishers and book-sellers, however, the privilege of posting the titles of their new books was specially reserved.

As printing became less expensive and methods for the mechanical reproduction of pictures and designs were discovered, it needed no great ingenuity to add emphasis to the poster by means of pictorial illustra-tion. Acrobats, the stall-keepers at fairs on the ice, and the like, were speedily induced to adorn their advertisements with rude drawings, while Royal proclamations were usually decorated heraldically. Early in the eighteenth century, the bills announcing the departure and arrival of coaches were headed by pictures, as for example the one which related to the Birmingham coach in 1731.

Even earlier in date, there are illustrated advertisements relating to the Roman Catholic church. One of these, produced in France, dated 1602, is very curious and elaborate in design. While, however, many posters such as this are profoundly interesting to the archæologist, they can hardly be considered works of art. It is not until the middle of the present century is reached that we find important examples of pictorial poster deliberately planned by an artist. The modern artistic poster movement, as we shall see in the next chapter, had its origin in Paris some fifty years ago.

CHAPTER II.

THE PICTORIAL POSTER IN FRANCE DURING THE PRESENT CENTURY.

As we have seen, the idea of the poster, and even of the pictorial poster, is an extremely ancient one, but it is only at the commencement of the present century that distinguished designers deliberately attempted to make the pictorial poster a work of art. The few posters, at once pictorial and artistic, which are of earlier date than the time in question, are artistic by accident rather than by deliberate intention. So early, however, as the year 1836, we find a really distinguished French artist, Lalance, producing a poster. Lalance was, perhaps, the pioneer of pioneers, and his advertisement for the book, " Comment Meurent Les Femmes," if not of great artistic interest, cannot be overlooked in any book dealing with the history of art as applied to the poster. Only a few copies exist. Immediately succeeding him, we have Célestin Nanteuil engaged in producing an advertisement for an edition of " Robert Macaire,"

dated 1837. The year following, Raffet
brought out his " Napoléon de Norvins."
This work is signed as well as dated.
Raffet, in addition to the " Napoléon de
Norvins," designed two more posters dealing with the career of the great emperor as
well as the history of Algeria. Very soon
after comes an important *affiche*, " Le
Prado," by Eugène Gauché, and from that
time the artistic poster became an established
institution.

It may be fairly stated that the direct
cause of the artistic poster in France was the
illustrated book. The illustrated book,
issued in weekly or monthly numbers, has
always appealed keenly to the French, and
it is usual to give the first number for nothing to all who care to ask for it. The
illustrators of these books were very frequently induced by the publishers of them
to do a poster advertising the edition of the
works they had illustrated. Sometimes one
of the illustrations in the book was merely
enlarged and lithographed, but more generally the artist made a special design. Perhaps, at the time, the most widely known
among French producers of the *affiche
illustré* was Gavarni. The vogue for the
works of this eminent illustrator and satirist
is perhaps not so great as it was twenty
years ago. At all events, the value of his
works is not nearly so great as it was then,
and it has become usual to talk of him in a

manner which is patronizing rather than
genuinely appreciative. It may be that his

DESIGN BY BERTRAND.

savage and grotesque point of view discounts his merits as an artist. His power
and originality, however, few will deny.

Among the posters which he designed, one
of the most characteristic is the "Œuvres
Choisis." The original is extremely rare,

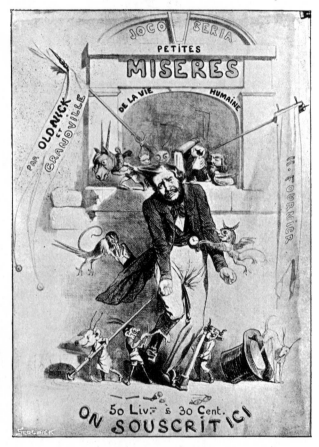

DESIGN BY GRANDVILLE.

but a copy exists in a folio volume in
the British Museum, in which one or two
other posters by Gavarni will be found.
For the "Almanach Imperial, 1846," by

Ste HELENE
TRANSLATION DES CENDRES
DE
L'EMPEREUR NAPOLEON

GIDE ÉDITEUR

5 RUE DES PAUSINS

DESIGN BY GRANDVILLE.

E. Marco de S. Hilaire, illustrated by Bertrand, a poster (which was, perhaps, an enlargement of the cover) exists. It is a very

DESIGN BY TONY JOHANNOT.

jingo affair, representing the French emperor standing on the globe with the imperial eagle of France at his feet. Of a little later

date are several interesting posters by
Grandville. Amongst them are " Les Meta-
morphoses du Jour " (of which a number

DESIGN BY TONY JOHANNOT.

of pigs in different costumes is the main
feature), " Des Animaux," " Ma Tante,"
" Petit Misère," and " St. Helène." Of the
two latter I need say nothing, since they are

C

reproduced here, save that they are included
in the collection of the British Museum.
An illustrated poster very characteristic of

DESIGN BY EDOUARD DE BEAUMONT.

its period, insomuch as it is intensely
grotesque, is the "Voyage ou il vous plaira,"
by Tony Johannot.   Its central figures are

a monstrous dwarf holding a lantern, a
crouching dragon, and an immense notice-
board. An *affiche* which is, perhaps, of

DESIGN BY T. H. FRÈRE.

even more general interest, is one done for
an illustrated edition of " Don Quichotte,"
in which the very perfect, gentle knight is

represented with a grotesqueness which
would certainly have astonished Cervantes
himself. Of a similar kind is the " Nains
Célèbres," by E. de Beaumont. An illustrated poster of a kind utterly different to
the one last discussed is by T. H. Frère.
It was designed for the advertisement of a
work entitled " La Touraine," by Stanislas
Bellanger de Tours. Under no circumstances should one overlook an *affiche* of
about the same period on account of the
great personality of its designer. It is very
generally admitted that the name of Edouard
Manet is one of the greatest in the history
of modern painting. It would indeed be
difficult to over-estimate the extent of his
influence on the pictorial art of the day. The
poster reproduced in these pages is not unworthy his great talent. It is curious to
notice that Manet and Fred. Walker, an
English artist of about the same time, as to
whose genius all are agreed, should have
been at one in their endeavour to make the
illustrated poster artistic as well as merely
pictorial.

I have not attempted to deal with any
save the most prominent of the great number of French designers who took part in
the poster movement during the fifties.
Their names and the titles of some of their
works will be found in the first catalogue of
M. Ed. Sagot, and valuable criticism is contained in the pages of M. Maindron.

CHAMPFLEURY – LES CHATS

DEUXIEME EDITION AVEC 52 DESSINS

DEUXIEME EDITION AVEC 52 DESSINS

Un volume illustré , Prix 5 Francs
En Vente ici.

DESIGN BY EDOUARD MANET.

CHAPTER III.

THE PICTORIAL POSTER IN FRANCE. THE WORK OF CHÉRET, GRASSET, AND TOULOUSE-LAUTREC.

So many contemporary French artists are designing posters, that a single chapter dealing with them all would be of an alarming length. I have therefore, in the first place, separated from their fellows three who seem to me curiously individual and worthy of careful consideration. Of the men whose names head this chapter, pre-eminence is due, for various reasons, to Jules Chéret, whose position, in the matter of poster-designing, is quite without parallel.

It may be that men of rarer, of more fascinating, talent have now and again devoted themselves to the *affiche ;* but none of them can compare with Chéret in the magnitude and curiosity of his achievement. Many have produced charming wall pictures : nobody, save Chéret, has made an emphatic mark on the aspect of a metropolis. Paris, without its Chérets, would be Paris without one of its most pronounced charac-

teristics; Paris, moreover, with its gaiety of
aspect materially diminished. The great
masses of variegated colour formed by
Chéret's posters greet one joyously as one
passes every hoarding, smile at one from the
walls of every café, arrest one before the
windows of every kiosque. The merits of
the Saxoléine lamp, the gaieties of the
Moulin Rouge, the charms of Loie Fuller,
the value of a particular brand of cough-
lozenges, are insisted upon with a good-
humoured vehemence of which Jules
Chéret alone appears to know the secret.
Others, in isolated cases, have possibly
achieved more compelling decorations, but
none can pretend to a success so uniform
and so unequivocal. Few men as richly
endowed with the gift of decoration would
have been content to produce work which,
were it not for the portfolio of the collector,
would be of an entirely ephemeral character.
It must be irritating to the artist to watch
the gradual destruction of his *chefs-d'œuvre*,
condemned as they are to be torn by every
wind, soaked by every shower, blistered by
the sun, blurred by the fog. It is natural
that he should turn his eyes longingly to the
comparative permanence of canvas, marble,
or bronze; and it says much for Chéret's
confidence in his artistic mission for his
nice realization of his possibilities and limitations, that he has remained faithful to the
affiche for over twenty years. Now and

DESIGN BY CHÉRET.

DESIGN BY CHÉRET.

add quality distinction, beauty

again, it is true, he has turned aside to do work of more universally recognized and more pretentious a character, and the very fact that he has touched scarcely anything which he has not adorned, emphasises his fidelity to a branch of art until quite recently despised and held of little moment. It is, indeed, mainly owing to this devotion, to this lavish expense of talent, that the poster is not even now considered beneath the *conclusion* dignity of the collector. The judicious, as soon as their eyes fell upon Chéret's vast lithographs, decided that he was no mere colour-printer's hack, but an artist whose work would have to be reckoned with. There was something positively alluring in the spectacle of a man who calmly placed his gift at the disposal of the tradesman, who accepted without murmur the limitations which the tradesman imposed upon him. It is possible that, had it not been for the circumstances of his life, the streets of Paris would have remained undecorated, so far as Chéret was concerned, to this day. Commencing as the humblest of lithographers, Chéret did not take up art of set intention, but passed irresistibly, though it may be unconsciously, into it. After long years of patient and tedious work as an ordinary lithographer, at the dawn of the year 1866, he commenced what was destined to be the most notable series of pictorial posters in existence, a series containing over

a thousand items, and one which happily
has yet to close. It is doubtless the conditions of his early life, the lessons learned
while under the yoke of trade, that have
enabled Chéret to appreciate to the full that
the first business of an advertisement is to
advertise. Avoiding, therefore, all subtle
harmonies, he goes in for contrasts of colour,
violent, it is true, but victorious in their
very violence. Blazing reds, hard blues,
glowing yellows, uncompromising greens,
are flung together, apparently haphazard,
but in reality after the nicest calculation,
with the result that the great pictures, when
on the hoardings, insist positively on
recognition. One might as well attempt to
ignore a fall of golden rain, as to avoid
stopping to look at them ; they are so many
riots of colour, triumphant in their certainty
of fascinating and bewildering the passer-
by.

As may be imagined, Chéret's skill has
fullest scope when dealing with the lightest
and gayest subjects : a *cascade de clowns*—
to borrow a phrase of Huysman—an en-
trance of ballet girls ; a joyous troupe of
children, contented because toy-laden; these,
and the like, are subjects most congenial to
him. His style is essentially the outcome
of the day. It possesses no decorative fore-
runners; it is not a thing derived; its parents
are the gaieties of modern Paris. It is intensely actual, and in its actuality lies, it

DESIGN BY CHÉRET.

seems to me, its greatest claim to consideration. It is infused with a somewhat hectic
gaiety which holds a not unimportant place
in the lives of us suffering from this "sick
disease of modern life." Of the sick disease
itself, Chéret gives no hint. He is un-
flagging in his vivacity, unswerving in his
insistence on the *joie de vivre;* instead of
pondering over the inevitable sorrow of
life, he busies himself depicting the naïve
grace of the child, the elegance of the
mondaine. His gifts lead him inevitably
to such subjects. His merit as a draughtsman lies, in part, in vivacious rather than
correct line : gaiety, as we have seen, is the
chief quality of his colour : his composition
is remarkable on account of the piquancy
and appropriateness of its detail. He chooses
with unerring fidelity the subjects suited
to his temperament and his gifts. These
subjects are not of infinite variety, and it
follows that if one sees a great quantity of
Chéret's work together, one becomes aware
of a certain feeling of monotony. One can
be satiated even of Chéret's gaiety and joyousness.

To attempt any account of Chéret's thousand and more posters, is obviously impossible in any but an elaborate monograph
devoted exclusively to him. I can do no
more here than comment on a few of the
most striking. It may be stated generally,
that while the earlier ones are rarest because

most difficult to procure, the more recent designs show the artist at his best. A mastery
of chromo-lithography such as his, cannot
be obtained without many essays, some of
which are foredoomed to failure. In addition, Chéret has gradually improved alike in
the splendour of his colour, and the disposal
of his pattern. Perhaps he has never been
happier in his treatment of children than in
one or two of the "Buttes-Chaumont" series.
The joy of the little ones in the possession of
their new playthings is contagious. Utterly
different in kind, though not less conspicuously successful, is "Les Coulisses de l'Opéra
au Musée Grevin," a delightfully piquant representation of a group of *premières danseuses*
in the traditional costume. As a specimen
of amazingly effective and strangely beautiful colour, it would be difficult to ex-
ceed the "Loïe Fuller" series; while, in the
matter of pert gracefulness, Chéret has done
nothing more delicious than the *chic* little
lady in the yellow dress who smiles at you
in the "Pantomimes Lumineuses." Anybody
who could resist her fascinations would be a
rival to St. Anthony. No collector of course,
will overlook the great series of *affiches*
which Chéret has contrived for the Folies
Bergère, the Moulin Rouge, the Alcazar
d'Eté, and similar places of amusement.

   In order to sum up his talent as a designer
of posters, Chéret has produced four decorative panels, which, although without letter-

DESIGN BY CHÉRET.

DESIGN BY CHÉRET (TOUR EIFFEL).

DECORATIVE PANEL, DESIGNED BY CHÉRET (COMEDY).

DECORATIVE PANEL, DESIGNED BY CHÉRET (PANTOMIME).

DECORATIVE PANEL, DESIGNED BY CHÉRET (MUSIC).

DECORATIVE PANEL, DESIGNED BY CHÉRET (DANCING).

ing, are posters to all intents and purposes,
and would take their places on a hoarding
quite admirably. The subjects are most
happily chosen; who, better than Chéret,
could symbolize, in manner light and fantastic, music, comedy, pantomime, and dancing? The designs gain immensely, insomuch as they are not disfigured with a legend,
for, in spite of the fact that the disposal of
the lettering is of the very essence of a poster,
Chéret, for some reason known only to himself, leaves that detail of his work to another
designer, with results by no means uniformly
fortunate. Before leaving Chéret, it is only
just to him to point out that his work loses
more than that of almost any other artist, in
the process of reproduction in black and
white. It is impossible to convey any idea
of his amazing colour by means of a half-
tone block, and therefore, fewer reproduc-
tions of his designs are included in these
pages than might be expected. Needless to
say, he suffers greatly from more or less un-
skilful imitators. For this reason, combined
with the fact that he is engaged on a series
of decorations for the Paris Hôtel de Ville,
his excursions into the art of the hoarding
will be less frequent than has been the case
hitherto.

To turn from Chéret to Eugène Grasset,
is to turn to an artist in whose art career the
poster is merely an incident. Grasset is a
paragon of versatility ; there are literally no

bounds to his comprehensiveness. Besides
being a painter of distinction, he has designed everything, from stained glass to
book-covers, from piano-cases to menus.
Unlike Chéret, he has been profoundly impressed by the work of old decorative designers ; he has certainly not disdained to
borrow ; his borrowings, however, have been
at once legitimate and intelligent. The
Japanese, the old Italians, and in a less
degree, the ancient Greeks, have been laid
under contribution, with results which, if
not amazingly original, are at least delightful. It would be idle to pretend that, from
the standpoint of the advertiser, Grasset is
the equal of Chéret. His sense of beauty,
his passion for decoration, make it impossible for him to achieve the daring and victorious colour which is so effective in the
work of Chéret. A panel of his posters,
side by side with a panel of those of Chéret,
is as a beautiful and somewhat quiet-hued
wall-paper to a cascade of flowers of every
conceivable colour. While, however, this is
an important matter from the advertiser's
point of view, it is of little moment to the
collector, whose primary object is to fill his
portfolios with things of beauty. At times,
indeed, Grasset does achieve irresistible
advertisement ; nobody, for instance, could
overlook the superb representation of Sarah
Bernhardt as " Jeanne d'Arc," standing with
splendid disdain amidst a forest of spears

DESIGN BY GRASSET.

E

EXPOSICIÓN
INTERNACIONAL
DE
MADRID
DE
1893

BAJO EL REGIO PATRONATO
DE SU MAJESTAD LA REINA REGENTE

DIRECCIÓN GENERAL:
PALACIO DE LA INDUSTRIA Y
DE LAS ARTES. MADRID

DESIGN BY GRASSET.

and a shower of arrows, and waving above
her head a great silken banner embroidered
with the *fleur-de-lis*. Again, one lingers
before the " Fêtes de Paris," attracted by its

DESIGN BY GRASSET FOR THE SALON DES CENT.

fine decorative qualities. Of an entirely
different kind is the delicious little poster
which the artist did for an exhibition of his
own work at the Salon des Cent in 1894 ;
in the naïve simplicity of the thing, com-

bined with its fine decorative quality, there
is a hint of Botticelli and the old Italians.
The contrast between this poster, slightly
archaic as it is, and the realistic "Odéon
Théatre" is complete. The latter represents
a charmingly graceful girl, in a delicious
modern gown, watching a play. She is
accompanied by a highly-proper looking
matron, whose self-importance is enhanced
by the possession of a handsome dress and
a wealth of jewels. Very pretty, again, is
the "Librairie Romantique," with the façade
of Nôtre Dame in the background. Less
worthy of Grasset is the "A la Place Clichy,"
which, in spite of the majestic old oriental
who descants on the merits of an elaborate
carpet to a critical European, is somewhat
commonplace. Among the other productions of this artist, some of them excellent,
but not calling for special description, are
the "Histoire de France," "Napoléon," "Chocolat Mexicain," and "L'Encre Marquet,"
as well as those done to advertise a work on
the capital cities of the world, and the exhibition of the productions of French decorative artists held in 1893 at the Grafton
Gallery. A bill designed for the South of
France Railway Company is curious, insomuch as it is unlike the other productions
of its designer. It consists of a series of
pleasant little landscapes wreathed in the
characteristic fruits and flowers of the
Riviera. The colour is striking and the

AFFICHE
EN
CHROMOTYPOGRAPHIE
exécutée
POUR le THÉÂTRE NATIONAL
DE
L'ODÉON
PAR
G. DE MALHERBE & H. CELLOT
Imprimeurs Editeurs
DES
NOUVELLES AFFICHES ARTISTIQUES
54. RUE NOTRE DAME DES CHAMPS
PARIS

DESIGN BY GRASSET.

DESIGN BY GRASSET.

poster full of sunshine. It is one of the
merits of Grasset that he is not, even in
what is to him so small a matter as poster-
designing, the slave of a single style,

DESIGN BY GRASSET FOR "L'ENCRE MARQUET."

although all his works are obviously from
the same hand. Before leaving him, it
should in fairness be stated that the lettering of his bills is ever appropriate and de-

lettering
grasset

corative.   True artist that he is, he neglects
no detail whatsoever ; in the smallest thing

DESIGN BY GRASSET ("CAPITAL CITIES").

as in the greatest, he is not merely scru-
pulous, but even fastidious.

It is no dispraise of Chéret and Grasset
to say that the work of Henri de Toulouse-
Lautrec is more fascinating than theirs.
The designs of the former two are alike in

DESIGN BY GRASSET FOR THE EXHIBITION HELD BY FRENCH
DECORATIVE ARTISTS AT THE GRAFTON GALLERY IN 1893.

that they are charming, though charming
in manner entirely different; Lautrec's productions, alluring and powerful as they are,
can by no stretch of the word be so de-

scribed.   He does not seek to attract you
by joyousness of colour or grace of pattern,
but rather to compel your attention by the
force of his realism or the curiosity of his
grotesqueness.   For his posters are at once
realistic and grotesque; they are delineations
of life as seen by a man who, possessing the
most acute powers of observation, is poig-
nantly impressed by the incongruities of
modern life, the physical peculiarities of
modern men.   He has some points of similarity with Hogarth, with Rowlandson, and
the like, but his art is quite non-moral ; he
has no mission to depict vice as either
hideous or ridiculous.   His extraordinary
" Reine de Joie," perhaps the most powerful,
and certainly the least agreeable, of his
posters, is a statement of fact rather than a
criticism.   This great bill, owing to the vehemence of the expression on the faces of the
three people it represents, to the wonderful
vigour of its line, to its extraordinarily effective, though simple, colour, is one of the
most powerful designs of the kind ever accomplished.   It may be doubted whether
any book has been advertised in so unforgettable a manner as *La Reine de Joie.*
For the Paris *café chantant* artiste who
possesses the charming name of Jane Avril,
this designer has devised a grotesque decoration, which could not fail imperiously to
call attention to her talents as a dancer.
Inspired it may be by her name, it may be

DESIGN BY TOULOUSE-LAUTREC.

by a happy accident, Lautrec has employed a
scheme of colour in which are found the pale

DESIGN BY TOULOUSE-LAUTREC.

sulphur hue of the primrose, the deeper
yellow of the daffodil, the crimson of the

F

tulip. Once having seen this work, the
name, and indeed something of the personality, of Jane Avril is impressed on one's
mind. Moreover, one easily recalls this un-
assuming poster vividly, when works of art,
consecrated by the admiration of generations
of critics, are quite forgotten, or only faintly
remembered. No man of more passionate
and curious talent than Aristide Bruant has
ever devoted himself to the business of light
amusement, and it was no doubt quite congenial to Lautrec to advertise the performances which he gives in his *cabaret*. Again,
the artist's picture of another entertainer,
Caudieux, represented in the act of quitting
the stage, is masterly for its indication of
movement and its powerful characterization.
Bad from the advertiser's point of view, but
most interesting from that of the collector,
is the extremely rare "Le Pendu," a production which for weird and intense tragedy
compares to advantage with any of the
artist's posters. Scarcely less rare, though
by no means so important, is the *affiche*
done to advertise the performances of La
Goulue at the Moulin Rouge. A far more
agreeable design is the "Divan Japonais,"
in which a fearful and wonderful girl, accompanied by a man as fashionable as he
seems to be imbecile, is represented under
the spell of Yvette Guilbert, whose tall,
thin figure is seen across the orchestra, her
arms, in the famous black gloves, being

DESIGN BY TOULOUSE-LAUTREC.

DESIGN BY TOULOUSE-LAUTREC.

DESIGN BY TOULOUSE-LAUTREC.

Confetti

Manufactured by J. & E. Bella, Charing Cross Rd. London. W.C.

imp. Bella & de Malherbe London & Paris

DESIGN BY TOULOUSE-LAUTREC.

crossed in front of her with characteristic nonchalance.

It is in no way astonishing that Mlle. Guilbert has strongly attracted Lautrec, and that he has frequently made her the subject of his work. No music-hall performer has, so far, approached this brilliant woman in ability or in artistic prestige. Like Patti and Sarah Bernhardt, she is implored to testify to the merits of every brand of soap or every new perfume; like them her reputation extends beyond the bounds of her native place, and she is the admired of several foreign capitals. If the flower of French art and literature assemble to honour Zola, the proceedings are incomplete without a song from her; if the fastidious De Goncourt is presented with the rosette of the Legion of Honour, what more fitting than that she should deliver a recitation ? In some degree she sees the life of modern Paris in the same light as Lautrec; her wonderful delineations are realistic as are his, though their realism is touched with a suspicion of the grotesque. Amongst other things, she has inspired Lautrec to a series of illustrations remarkable alike in drawing and colour; and he has not disdained to design lithographs to adorn the covers of different items of her *répertoire*. Owing to his kindness, I am enabled to reproduce, as the frontispiece to this volume, a sketch for a poster which he designed for her, but which, unfor-

tunately, has never got beyond the experimental stage.   It seems to me a specially
interesting example of a remarkable talent
applied to a very congenial subject. The
posters of Lautrec are something more than
works of art; they are human documents
strangely eloquent of their moment. For
this reason, their value may be more permanent than that of the productions either
of Chéret or Grasset, delightfully fantastic as
are the former, charmingly decorative as are
the latter.

CHAPTER IV.

THE POSTER IN FRANCE: THE WORK OF WILLETTE, FORAIN, STEINLEN, ANQUETIN, BONNARD, IBELS, VALLOTON, DE FEURE, AND MÉTIVET.

It is not for a moment to be pretended that the artists with whom this chapter deals are in any sense members of a single school: they have, indeed, many more points of difference than of similarity. I deal with them together, because, speaking roughly, their designs are saturated with the spirit of the day: their decorations are realistic, rather than fantastic or picturesque. They lean towards Lautrec, rather than towards Chéret or Grasset, but they are in no sense his imitators; some of them, indeed, are actually his predecessors.

Willette is an artist of such astonishing facility and variety, that he has, comparatively speaking, devoted little time to the *affiche*, and save in one or two conspicuous instances, he has failed to achieve compelling advertisements. And yet his artistic personality is so curious and so powerful that his posters are nearly all interesting to the

collector,—more interesting to the collector,
it may well be, than satisfactory to the
advertiser. Willette is master of several
manners. He can be realistic to the point
of brutality, symbolical, graceful ; while now
and then he is almost austerely classical.
There are, happily, few posters so impreg-
nated with race hatred as the anti-Semitic
bill intended to forward the artist's can-
didature at the *Elections législatives* of the
22nd of September, 1889. The design is
ugly in the last degree, but it is, nevertheless, strangely powerful. Very different and
very much more pleasing is the lithograph
in black—admirably composed and executed
—which advertised the successful pantomime, entitled *L'Enfant Prodigue*. The
design is at once graceful and dramatic,
and it is not surprising that a proof before
letters is one of the gems of a collection of
the posters of Willette. No more interesting
souvenir of an experiment which fascinated
both Paris and London can be conceived.
Again, the bill advertising the International
Exhibition of Commerce and Industry, held
some time ago at the Champs de Mars (an
unlettered proof of which commands no less
than two pounds), is very desirable. The
little bill in colours bearing the legend,

> " Ainsi qu'un papillon volage,
> A qui passe aujourd'hui, demain sera passé.
> Laisse-toi cuellir au passage
>   Papillon d'Actualité,"

DESIGN BY WILLETTE.

DESIGN BY WILLETTE.

DESIGN BY WILLETTE.

prenez du Cacao
Van Houten

DESIGN BY WILLETTE.

DESIGN BY WILLETTE.

is pretty, alike in colour and pattern, and
has already become rare.

Entirely appropriate to its purpose is the
" Nouveau Cirque" advertisement, in which
clowns, bare-back riders, and performing
animals of all kinds—from a frog to an
elephant—disport themselves with the utmost *abandon.* From this to the " Cacao
Van Houten," is a far cry. From the point
of view of the advertiser, Willette has done
nothing better than his life-size study of a
Dutch waitress in national costume. The
thing is very decorative, and succeeds admirably in attracting attention : another and
more complicated design for the same firm
is only a shade less successful. This is
entitled " La loi défendent le cacao contre le
chocolat." The other posters of this artist
include the rare " Petite National," the
"Evénement Parisien" (which was, I believe,
suppressed), the " Courrier Française," the
" Exposition Charlet," and the " Elysée
Montmartre." The posters of Willette are
marked by variety and ingenuity of invention, and there is little doubt that they will
be of permanent value as revelations of a
talent as individual as it is powerful.

If the artistic poster is an unimportant
incident in the career of Willette, it is still
more so in that of Forain, whose essays in
this direction have been few and far between.
Forain is known to nearly every artist in
Europe as a great master of black and white.

Few, if any, can approach him in technical dexterity, few can express so much in so few lines. Moreover, to his technical mastery is added a searching power of criticism which gives to his work a further, and a most important, interest. In his desire to depict the truth, the whole truth, and nothing but the truth, he (no doubt unconsciously) becomes a moralist. He depicts life from no sentimental point of view; he can be realistic without seeming to appreciate the tragedy which is of the very essence of realism, so that on seeing one of his illustrations of modern life, one receives, apart from technical delight, a distinctly literary impression. Of his posters, perhaps the earliest is one unsigned and without lettering, representing an illuminated garden, in which a woman is depicted in the midst of an explosion of fireworks. Subsequent to this comes a bill to advertise one of the novels of Dubut de Laforest, which bears the artist's signature. The design which announces Forain's political drawings for the " Figaro " is of slight importance, as it was not originally intended for a poster. In spite of this it is by no means easy to meet with. Of greater interest is the " Exposition des Arts de la Femme." It was, however, only when Forain received a commission to produce an illustrated advertisement for a cycle show that he achieved a really memorable poster, a poster of real charm and rare

PALAIS DE L'INDUSTRIE

Août·Novembre

Exposition
DES
ARTS DE LA FEMME

LA
PARISIENNE
DU
SIÈCLE

7 Dioramas par
Poilpot

DESIGN BY FORAIN.

DESIGN BY FORAIN.

originality. The sport of bicycling seems to have fascinated the *Parisienne* completely, and Forain has made a charming design, in which she is depicted in complete enjoyment of the fashionable pastime. The colour scheme is restrained and delicate, and the production, which exists in two sizes, should certainly be found amongst the treasures of every amateur of the *affiche*.

The somewhat risky pages of the *Gil Blas Illustré* have for a considerable time been noticeable to artists, chiefly on account of a series of coloured illustrations by Stein-len. His relentless veracity in depicting the life of the lower classes of the Paris of to-day is almost without rival. No detail of squalor seems to escape him; without a tinge of remorse he proceeds to inform us of the meanest incidents in the tragedy of the poor or vicious quarters of the great city. By reason of a certain emphasis of colour and crudeness of design the art of Steinlen is admirably adapted to the production of such human documents. But it cannot be main-tained that, whatever their technical merits, these studies of human misery are other than unpleasant—even painful. It is, therefore, altogether agreeable, when one turns to his essays in the art of the poster, to find his work graceful rather than tragic, urbane rather than mordant. Forsaking his mission of realistic illustration, he becomes gay, dainty, and fanciful as the best of his fel-

lows. Even in a higher degree than the
majority of them, he makes his design appropriate to the thing advertised. His decorations are spiced with a certain actuality, and,
in being so, insist more effectively on the
particular article the merits of which it is
their business to proclaim. No better example of this could, I think, be put forward
than the " Lait pur de la Vingeanne stérilisé,"
a design which, in view of the material to
be advertised, is conceived in the happiest
vein. The pretty little girl drinking the
milk, so much coveted of the cats which
surround her, is less interesting than the
animals themselves. The draughtsmanship
of the latter is excellent, while there is a
hint of that humanity of expression about
the creatures which has produced for the work
of Landseer so immense a popularity. Not
less admirable, and of still greater interest,
is the poster designed to advertise the performances of Yvette Guilbert at the Ambassadeurs. Amongst the numerous artists
to whom the Sarah Bernhardt of the music-
halls has given commissions none has been
more successful than Steinlen. The poster
represents the singer behind the footlights
in an attitude pre-eminently characteristic.
The thing does not amount to a caricature,
as does the hitherto unpublished delineation
of Toulouse-Lautrec, but is merely a slightly
exaggerated portrait. It is remarkably sug-
gestive of a most alluring and delightful

DESIGN BY STEINLEN, USED IN FRANCE FOR A POSTER FOR THE
"LAIT PUR DE LA VINGEANNE STÉRILISÉ," AND IN ENGLAND
FOR NESTLÉ'S SWISS MILK.

H

DESIGN BY STEINLEN.

personality. As an advertisement, it must
be confessed, it is not all that could be
desired. The colour scheme, while very
dainty, is not one which insists on its pre-
sence on the hoardings, so that the proximity
of (for example) a Chéret renders it to some
extent ineffective. At the same time, it is
one of the most charming designs of the
kind in existence, and no collector should
fail to possess himself of a copy. It exists
in three states : proofs before letters pulled
in two tints only, ordinary proofs before
letters, and prints after letters. In the
former state it is rapidly increasing in value,
but, insomuch as the lettering is of the essence of the design, the final state is the most
desirable of all. To advertise an exhibition
of his own work, Steinlen produced another
study of cats, which is almost as agreeable as
the " Lait pur." It is in two states : proofs
before and after letters. The artist's design
for the watering-place, Vernet-les-Bains, is
not very important, but his early " Mothu
et Doria," in three states, should not be
overlooked. Earlier in date than any of the
designs I have discussed is the " Trouville "
and " Le Rêve." The latter is a pretty
composition reproduced in chromotypo-
gravure. While the posters of Steinlen are
not so striking on the hoarding as those of
some of his contemporaries, they are of the
highest artistic interest, and will no doubt
take a place second to none in the affections

of many collectors.) It is significant that
already the rarest of them are by no means
easy to procure.

The art of Ibels is as little comprised in
the poster as that of Steinlen. (It is happily
characteristic of young artists of the present
day, both here and in France, that painting
is not the only god of their æsthetic adora-
tion : they experiment in many mediums,
and it is really remarkable in how great a
number of such experiments they succeed.)
What is generally true, is especially so of
H. G. Ibels.   Like Grasset, he has held an
exhibition of his pictures at the Salon des
Cent; he has made his mark in the galleries
of the Champs de Mars; he has designed
the covers of several pieces of music, and
of a volume of poems by his brother, entitled
"Chansons Colorées"; in addition, he is well-
known as a book illustrator.   His point of
view is somewhat akin to that of Toulouse-
Lautrec : he is passionately interested in his
own moment, and depicts modern life with
similar insistence on its ugly and grotesque
aspects.   And yet Ibels rarely fails to be
decorative, and his style is the outcome of
his own artistic personality, rather than the
result of study of the work of other men.
In his posters he has been conspicuously
successful ; so much so, that it is difficult
to point to a single failure, though, it must
be remembered, that as yet his productions
have not been very numerous.   It is possible

DESIGN BY IBELS.

DESIGN BY IBELS.

that with some the "Mévisto à l'Horloge" will be deemed his best design, but it can in no sense be considered his most original. It represents the actor as Pierrot, and is graceful and pleasing rather than characteristic; indeed, one would almost think that in designing it the artist had been at pains to conceal his personality. Nor is the " Salon des Cent"—a charming and delicate little lithograph—in spite of the ingenuity and fantasy of its grouping of Pierrot, Harlequin and Columbine, the most noteworthy of Ibels' posters. We see him at his most original, in an advertisement for the illustrated paper entitled "l'Escarmouche," to which he, together with Lautrec, Vuillard, Willette, and Anquetin, contributed drawings. It represents a *café* of the lower class, such as abounds in the workmen's quarter of Paris. The enormously fat *patron* enthroned behind the metal-topped bar, the waitress, cloth in hand, clad in her slovenly dress, the *ouvriers* in typical blue blouses, are studies in which accurate portraiture has been but slightly sacrificed to grotesqueness. The whole scene is admirably conceived, and the colour scheme, though very restrained, is certainly telling. Those who can do so should secure a proof before letters of this work, for the lettering is, I believe, not by the artist himself, and mars the effect of the design, although not in a very marked degree. Another interesting

bill is that done for Mévisto's performances
at the Scala music-hall; this is of great
size and striking originality. But if grotesque force, and the power of reducing
scenes of modern lower-class life into
decoration, are Ibels' most pronounced
characteristics, he can produce posters of
the suavest charm. Amongst all the *affiches*
I know, none seems to me more delightful
than this artist's "Irène Henry." The
café chantant singer whom it represents is
justly a popular favourite with the Parisian
public from the fact that she infuses into
her performances no small amount of personality; moreover, her art is marked by
grace and finish. Those who would see
her as she appears to audiences at the
Horloge, without going there, have only to
look at Ibels' poster. With the rarest
felicity, he has caught her physical individuality. She is represented in the act of
singing in the open air to a crowd in the
café, lighted by the familiar circle of white
lamps. The line of the figure is most expressive : violet is the predominating colour.
This poster is worthy a place in the French
music hall series, which includes those
designed by Lautrec for Jane Avril, by
Steinlen for Yvette Guilbert, and by an
artist whom I am about to consider, Anquetin, for Marguerite Dufay.

So far as I know, Anquetin has only produced two *affiches* of importance, but each

DESIGN BY IBELS.

Tous les Soirs

Irène Henry

à l'Horloge

DESIGN BY IBELS.

of them is worthy of the closest attention.
The design for Marguerite Dufay is a piece
of triumphant vulgarity. The subject is a
very simple one; it is merely a woman of
almost impossible fatness who performs
at various Parisian music-halls on the trom-
bone. Having stated this, one has, however,
given no idea of the extraordinary qualities
of this bill. It is safe to say that, once seen,
it will never be forgotten; it should have
made the fortune of the performer whom it
advertises. The mirth of the thing is victorious and infectious; one seems almost to
hear the coarse laugh; the ample body in
the green dress seems to move as one stares
at it. In line, in movement, this poster is,
from a certain point of view, a veritable
masterpiece. An advertisement which is, it
seems to me, altogether more worthy of
Anquetin's great talent is one designed for
" Le Rire," a recently issued journal. It is
an extremely fine lithograph in a single printing, and, as at present it can be procured for
a few shillings, it should be in the possession, not only of those who care for posters as
such, but also of all who are amateurs of
the beautiful art of lithography. In the foreground is the figure of a huge man in
mediæval costume, which, while touched
with the grotesque, is splendidly flamboyant.
At his side he carries a large portfolio,
adorned with a grinning mask, while his
hands, which are admirably drawn, point

towards a crowd of grinning pigmies beneath
him. Every one of the crowd is extremely
expressive, and the effect of the whole production is enhanced by very excellent lettering. It would be difficult to meet with
two *affiches* more interesting than the
" Marguerite Dufay " and " Le Rire," and
they place Anquetin amongst the masters
of the art of the poster.

If Anquetin is an artist of marked originality, so, in a manner totally different, is
Pierre Bonnard. Save in the small number
of his posters, he resembles Anquetin in
hardly anything ; on the other hand, his
work has points of similarity with the later
work of Lautrec. The posters of both these
artists are decorative in a curious and somewhat similar sort of way, decorative in spite
of their marked grotesqueness. Between
the " Confetti " of Lautrec and the " Revue
Blanche " of Bonnard there is a distinct
decorative affinity. As both of them are
dated the same year, 1894, it is needless to
suggest that either of these intensely personal artists has derived anything from the
other ; there is, indeed, no evidence whatsoever of imitation, or even influence. Of the two
best-known posters of Bonnard, the " France
Champagne " is the earlier in point of time,
having been published in 1891. It is a
lithograph in three colours, and represents
an extraordinarily fantastic, and extremely
décolletée girl, who holds in one hand a

DESIGN BY ANQUETIN.

DESIGN BY BONNARD.

DESIGN BY BONNARD.

DESIGN BY VALLOTON.

closed fan, and in the other an overflowing
glass of champagne,which tumbles about her
in a great cascade of foam. The background
is yellow and the girl's dress red, while
the upper part of the design is occupied
by the arms of Paris and the text in large
letters. The draughtsmanship is curious and
vivacious, and the colouring conspicuously
successful. This poster is not large, mea-
suring as it does, only thirty-two by twenty-
nine inches. The " Revue Blanche," though
of nearly the same size, is much more complicated. In the foreground is a woman in
huge hat and cape, which partly conceal her
face, at whom an extraordinarily grotesque
street urchin points his finger. The background is composed of innumerable advertisements of the *revue*, which a man in a
great coat and silk hat, with his back to the
spectator, is reading attentively. All the
figures are in a sort of slate colour. The
legend is admirably introduced into the foreground by means of huge white letters.
Owing to the curiosity of its decoration,
this specimen of Bonnard's work is a most
desirable possession for the collector.

It has been the good fortune of Valloton
to produce at least one poster which is excellent from every point of view. Nothing
more appropriate to the advertisement of a
frivolous burlesque than his " Ah ! la Pé .
la Pé, la pépinièré " could well be imagined.
It represents a characteristic audience at a

theatre convulsed with laughter at what is taking place on the stage. The variety of expression on the faces of the spectators is infinite, and the effect of the whole thing is as mirthful as may be. From the advertiser's point of view, I can conceive nothing more completely satisfactory. It exists in colours and in black, and the latter is the rarer. The same artist's " Carte de Paris " would seem already to have become scarce. It is a large lithograph in one colour; an example was shown at the Poster Exhibition at the Royal Aquarium. There is also a large address card designed by Valloton for M. Sagot. While this is not actually a poster it almost amounts to one, and were it to be executed on a large scale, it would doubtless be most successful. It is to be hoped that Valloton, encouraged by his universally recognized success in the art of the poster, will not altogether give up its practice in favour of those other branches of art in which he is distinguished.

The style of De Feure, if not so well adapted to poster work as that of some of his contemporaries, is nevertheless very interesting. His most characteristic effort is, perhaps, the "Salon des Cent, 5ᵉ Exposition." This design is very modern and very fantastic. It exists in three states— proofs before letters on vellum, proofs on Japanese paper, and ordinary prints. The proofs before letters command very good

ENTRÉE
o,50cts

5me EXPOSITION
du 1er au 31 Octobre

SALON DES CENT 31 Rue Bonaparte

DESIGN BY DE FEURE.

DESIGN BY DE FEURE.

DESIGN BY DE FEURE.

DESIGN BY MÉTIVET.

prices. Amongst the other posters of De Feure is that done for the performance of the singer, Edmée Lescaut, at the Casino de Paris; for the newspaper "Le Diablotin"; and for the "Paris Almanach." In addition, we must not overlook the pleasant little design for the contents bill of a special issue of "To-Day."

The posters of Lucien Métivet are of very unequal merit. On the one hand the designs done by him for Eugénie Buffet, in her realistic *répertoire* of songs, are extremely distinguished. While, on the other, I could point to examples by this artist which are utterly unworthy his talent. Amongst Métivet's earlier works are "La Famille, journal hebdomadaire illustré," and "L'Hygiène." A more recent bill advertises "Les Joyeuses commères de Paris," but Métivet's talent is seen at its best in the Eugénie Buffet advertisements, two studies worthy a place amongst the best posters which have come from the hands of contemporary French artists.

CHAPTER V.

THE PICTORIAL POSTER IN FRANCE: THE WORK OF GUILLAUME, PALEOLOGUE, CHOUBRAC, BOUTET DE MONVEL, AMAN-JEAN, SCHWÆBE, SINET, JOSSOT, MAYET, AND OTHER ARTISTS.

PROMINENT among the French designers of posters with whom I have not previously dealt is Guillaume, an artist widely known in England by reason of the admirable illustrations which, from time to time, appear in our periodicals. Save Chéret and Choubrac, few artists have done so much poster work as Guillaume, and not many have maintained so high a level of accomplishment. Vigour, vivacity, and high spirits, rather than beautiful design and fine colour, are the characteristic qualities of posters by Guillaume. He is, it seems to me, seen at his best in the admirable " Extrait de Viande Armour," which is reproduced here. In its way, and looking to the thing to be advertised, nothing better has been done. The

gigantic " strong man," with his huge torso,
colossal arms and legs, holding a tiny tea-
cup in his immense hands, is not easily forgotten.   The expression on the man's face
is inimitable, and the accessories, such as
cannons and dumbbells, are most appropriately chosen.) The " Chapeaux 1 elion "
is a more complicated design, representing
a crowd of men wearing hats of every conceivable shape.   The colour of this design
is very good, but its chief merit lies in the
facial expression of the different members
of the crowd.   It would be impossible to
conceive any single person in a hat other
than the one he is wearing.   In another
excellent poster we are presented with a
very *fin-de-siècle* young lady riding astride
a stork which bears her rapidly through
space.   It would be hopeless to attempt
anything like a complete list of Guillaume's
posters, but among the most recent are the
following, all of which deserve the attention
of the collector : " Dentifrices du Dr. Bonn,"
" Gigolette," " Old England," " Le Pôle
Nord," "Cycles Vincent fils," "Le Vin d'Or"
(in two sizes, unsigned), " Parfumerie Diaphane ; le Diaphane Sarah Bernhardt,"
" L'œuvre de Rabelais par J. Garnier," and
" Ducreux et Giralduc (Ambassadeurs) ".

Although a Frenchman, the work of Jean
de Paleologue, or " Pal," as he is more frequently called, is perhaps better known to
the Londoner than to the Parisian.   His

DESIGN BY GUILLAUME.

DESIGN BY GUILLAUME.

DESIGN BY GUILLAUME.

DESIGN BY GUILLAUME.

bright and flippant posters can be seen any
day on the London hoardings, and I have,
therefore, purposely selected for reproduction two examples in his less usual manner.
The "Lucile Wraïm" is of an elegance to
which Paleologue does not often attain, and
would be distinguished in almost any
collection of posters. "The Euskal Jai
Parisien," besides being a good advertisement, is curious on account of its subject.
Collectors who would possess a more typical
example of Paleologue's work would be well
advised to secure one or more of his music-
hall series or his "Cabourg," an advertisement for the watering-place of that name.
It is a large lithograph in five colours, and
represents a very charming lady who, while
bathing, is bent upon displaying her charms
to the utmost. While Paleologue can in
no sense be compared to Chéret in his gift
of diffusing joyousness and gaiety, his
work is undoubtedly "chic," and rarely
fails in its first business of advertisement.
Some of his posters have become difficult to
procure, notably one designed for a Drury
Lane pantomime some few years since.

No artist, save Jules Chéret, has been
more indefatigable in the making of posters
than Choubrac. The list given in M.
Maindron's book is a long one; that given
in the catalogues of M. Sagot is still longer.
The posters of Choubrac do not seem to
have received so much attention at the hands

of collectors as those of some of his better-
known contemporaries.   At the same time,
not a few of them are interesting and rare.
The bill done for the " Fin de Siècle " was
suppressed, and, as a consequence, is in
great demand.   It exists in four states,
three of which, in good condition, command
no less than fifty francs.   Merely to give
the names of the music-halls and theatres
for which Choubrac has worked would take
up the better part of a page, while a list of
the *artistes* whom he has advertised would
be still longer.   Amongst the most noticeable of his recent bills are the following :
" Eldorado.   Y'a pas d'erreur," " Folies
Bergère.   Armand Ary," " Folies Bergère.
Programme," " Folies Dramatiques.   Miss
Robinson," " Moulin Rouge.   Au Joyeux,"
" Neuilly-sur-Seine.   Fête des fleurs," and
" Gaieté.   Rosa et Josepha " (in two states).
    An artist more unlike Choubrac than
Maurice Boutet de Monvel it would be
assuredly impossible to find, and the fact
that these names are in juxtaposition must
be taken as proof that no systematic arrangement has been attempted in this chapter.
Boutet de Monvel is a painter of European
reputation.   His fame as an illustrator for,
and a delineator of, children stands very high.
His studies of child-life are unlike those of
any other artist.   They display the keenest
observation and, as Mr. Pennell has rightly
observed, one finds in them not a line with-

DESIGN BY PALEOLOGUE.

DESIGN BY PALEOLOGUE.

out meaning. Boutet de Monvel has, I
believe, produced only three posters. Two
of them are among the most charming
things seen on the Paris hoardings for

DESIGN BY BOUTET DE MONVEL.

many a long day. Both of these are comparatively small. That which is earlier in
date, "Petite Poucette," was originally
designed as a cover for a piece of music,

but, when reproduced on a larger scale, was
found to be thoroughly effective as a poster.
More dainty, if not more characteristic of
the art of Boutet de Monvel, is the " Pâte
Dentifrice du Dr. Pierre." In this design,
one of the prettiest and most delightful
little ladies in the whole Monvel gallery of
pretty little ladies insists on the merit of
the tooth-paste which, if it be half as good
as she is charming, must be excellent indeed. Every artist knows his own business
best, but one can only hope that, in what
leisure he can snatch from his work in paint
and illustration, Boutet de Monvel will
place the collector of posters under new
obligations to him. His note as a decorator
of the hoardings is as distinct as it is agreeable.

A very interesting figure in modern
design is undoubtedly Carloz Schwæbe.
One of the leading lights of that curious
institution the " Salon Rose + Croix,"
it would indeed be curious if Schwæbe did
anything commonplace. His posters are
as remarkable as those other productions
with which he has delighted some and
puzzled not a few. Mystic, slightly archaic,
they are the work of a man of poetical temperament who has chosen the graphic arts
instead of literature as his means of expression. The two posters from his hand are
very decorative in their strange way, and
contain passages of great beauty. In the

DESIGN BY BOUTET DE MONVEL.

"Audition d'Œuvres de Guillaume Lekeu,
Salle d'Harcourt," the face of the fantastic

DESIGN BY CARLOZ SCHWÆBE.

kneeling woman is remarkably impressive,
while the irises amidst which she kneels are

beautifully drawn. The lettering of this
poster is most original, and the designer
has evidently taken great pains with it.   It
is a lithograph in two colours, and measures
forty-two and a half by thirty-one and a
half inches. Schwæbe's larger poster, the
" Salon Rose + Croix," is in one colour
only, and is a good example of his work.
So far this curiously-gifted artist has confined himself to advertising a concert and
a picture show ; it is not to be expected
that he will ever condescend to soap or
extract of beef. Another of the Rose +
Croix men, Aman-Jean, has done a poster
for the Salon which rivals in curiosity the
productions of Schwæbe himself.

A little advertisement which had, it may
well be, some influence on the poster movement in England, was that by which André
Sinet advertised an exhibition of his own
works held at the Goupil Gallery in 1893.
This was an attractive little bit of design of
which the colour was very agreeable.   In
addition to it, Sinet has done the inevitable poster for Yvette Guilbert. Another
painter of talent who has made an advertisement for an exhibition of his own work is
H. Guérard. It represents a group of
ravens and is in poker work. It would
appear to be rare, as it is quoted in none of
the catalogues. A copy, exhibited at the
Aquarium in 1894, is in the collection of
Mr. Ernest Hart. Still another artist who

UNLETTERED DESIGN (IN POKER WORK) FOR A POSTER, BY H. GUÉRARD.

DESIGN BY CAZOLY.

DESIGN BY GRÜN.

M

DESIGN BY H. GRAY.

has, I believe, done only one poster, is Goissaud. His design was to advertise the " Société des miniaturistes et enlumineurs de France," and is a lithograph in one colour. Among the Salon des Cent series we have, besides the admirable posters of Grasset and Ibels already alluded to, a very grotesque and effective little design by Jossot. It represents an amazing old gentle- man of weird aspect, in cocked hat, pay- ing his franc for admission to the exhibi- tion. Of its kind it is effective enough. Another, by Cazoly, with a curious portrait of Paul Verlaine is reproduced here.

It is certainly with no view to hurt the feelings of those artists whose names do not head this chapter that they are represented by a mere *et cetera*. It must be understood that one of the least polite of contractions, in this case, involves no discourtesy whatsoever.

For example, I may instance such able work as Grün's "Le Carillon : cabaret artis- tique." Few posters are more vivid or more actual than this. The price of it is a matter of pence, and it should certainly not be neglected by those whom it amuses to col- lect the *affiche illustré.* Grün, in addition to " Le Carillon," has produced " Poléon- Revue : Décadent's Concert," and in addi- tion a design for an insurance company. One of the most charming of the more recent French posters is one by H. Gray, dealing with " La Prétentaine," a play produced some time ago at the Nouveau Théâtre. In addition he has advertised " La Bonita " at the Cirque d'Eté, " Les Mousquetaires," at the same place, " Les Saltimbanques " at the Cirque d'Hiver, and the *bal masqué* at the Théâtre de l'Opéra. The last is perhaps the best known of his *affiches*. Among others, Bac has done a poster for Yvette Guilbert at the Horloge, which is signed and dated 1892. The bicycling craze has called into existence a perfect torrent of posters, and Bac, together with Gray, Guillaume, Lunel, and Paleologue, have produced posters of more or less interest. A gentleman who is sufficiently modest not to state his name, did a design which called forth the wrath of the authorities. Whereupon an artist called Lepur designed an *affiche* bearing the significant legend, of which this is a translation : " Grand choice of vine-leaves (fig-leaves) of all sizes for posters, as demanded by the virtuous journals, the ' T(emps '), the ' G(aulois '), and the ' D(ébats ')."

The following is a list, with the names of typical examples of their work, of some other French artists of distinction who have designed posters : Barbizet (" La branche cassée "), Bouisset (F.) (" Bazar de l' Hôtel-de-Ville," " Exposition de jouets," " Chocolat Menier "), Desicy (H.) (" Un héritage, roman "), Dutriac ("Ambassadeurs: Danseuses Espagnols "), Faria (" Ba-ta-clan:

DESIGN BY OGÉ.

Paulus"), Dufay ("Portrait,") (" Les Rey Nol's)," Galice (G.) ("Concert parisien: Esther Lekain," "Fête des Fleurs," "Paulan Brébion," "Scala: Jeanne Bloch"), Guydo ("Eldorado: Aimée Eymard"), Honer ("Concert parisien: Bonnaire"), Hope ("Gaieté: Tour de Nesle"), Huvey ("Grasside"), Lamy (L.) (" Le capitaine Henriot, opéra comique," "Théâtre national lyrique"), Lebégue (L.) ("Bals travestes et tableaux vivants"), Lefèvre (L.) ("Cacao lacté," "Electricine," "L'hiver à Nice"), Levy (E.) ("Châtelet Michel Strogoff," "Cirque d'Hiver: Caravane dans le désert," "Folies Bergère: Vue de la salle," "Petit national: Le prince Mouffetard"), Meunier (G.) ("Papier à cigarettes Job," "Parfumerie Edéa," "Le Sahara à Paris: Champ de Mars"), Truchet (A.) ("Cabaret des Quat'z' Arts," "Eldorado: Alice Berthier.")

It will have been noticed already how great a part the music-hall and the *café chantant* play in the history of the pictorial poster. Yvette Guilbert has been the cause of a baker's dozen of *affiches;* Anna Thibaud (that charming singer of the songs of Béranger); Anna Held, with her curious manner, and still more curious appearance; Irène Henri, of intense personality; Jane Avril, and May Belfort; to say nothing of Aristide Bruant, of Caudieux, of Paulus, and the rest of the school who have made the music-hall stage of France a matter of no small importance

DESIGN BY GASTON NOURY.

in her social life, have been favourite subjects of the designers of posters. It has
always been held that the career of an actor,
in consideration of its evanescence, is not

DESIGN BY VERNEUIL.

without a certain pathos. It is true that
we remember, through the gossip of their
friends, Garrick and Mrs. Siddons, Talma
and Rachel, but even these are uncertain

phantoms lingering in the haze of memory.
Only yesterday they were intensely actual,
to-day they are not more real than Bur-
bage and Betterton. After all, the history
of the actor's art is not without its im-
mortals. Macaulay's schoolboy could doubtless have related the compliment of Dr.
Johnson to Mrs. Siddons : the latest esca-
pade of the great Sarah is the joy of the
paragrapher. The music-hall, however, has
still no artist in any country (save, perhaps,
the unforgettable Yvette) who has much
chance of permanent remembrance. But
when the toil and moil of existence is ended,
when the singer has sung his last song, it
may chance that he will be remembered
because some collector of such unconsidered
trifles as picture posters has placed in his
portfolio a work of Chéret or of Lautrec.

To turn from the music-halls to the great
railway companies is an emphatic transi-
tion, and yet the former, no less than the
latter have done much to encourage the
artist to apply his talent to the *affiche*. The
Great Western Railway Company have
illustrated at their stations and in their
carriages, by means of photography, all that
is romantic and interesting in the country
through which their line runs. And, again,
the great lines of the United States have
brought into vogue vast systems of pictorial
advertisement. Their opportunity was undoubtedly a magnificent one. For subject

DESIGN BY GAUSSON.

DESIGN BY L. LEFÈVRE.

matter they had some of those vast natural developments which appeal to mere man as absolutely terrific. The waterfall, splashing itself into luminous dust, the immense and silent mountains, the lakes which are seas, the vasty cañons which occur in different parts of the States, inevitably appeal to the imagination. It is therefore not wonderful that the great lines of America have preferred literal and exact illustration to fantastic delineation. The railways of France, on the other hand, have employed to no inconsiderable extent the artist to figure the beauties of the places at which they have stations. Amongst the most important French designers who have worked at the railway *affiche* are :—Fraipont (G.) : (" Chemin de fer de l'Etat : Bains de mer de Royan " : " Royan sur l'Océan," " Chemin de fer d'Orléans : Excursions en Touraine " : " Excursions en Touraine et aux châteaux des bords de la Loire," " Chemin de fer de l'Ouest : Argenteuil à Mantes," " Cie de l'Ouest et de Brighton : Fleurs, fruits, primeurs à destination de Londres," " Paris à Londres (L'Angleterre et l'Ecosse) " " Chemin de fer du Nord : Excursions à la mer," " Chemin de fer de l'Est : Royat," " Chemin de fer de l'Ouest : Bretagne, Normandie," " Normandie et Bretagne," " Chemin de fer de l'Ouest à Brighton : Paris à Londres," " Chemin de fer du Nord : Anvers, Exposition univer-

N

selle.") Ochoa: (" Club Train," " Mediter-
ranée," " Express (Cie Int. des wagons-lits),"
" Orient-Express," " Peninsular-Express ").
Hugo d'Alési (*affiches simili-aquarelles*):
" Paris, Lyons - Marseilles, Algérie,"
"Genève," " L'hiver à Nice," (two subjects),
" Lac de Thoune," " Mont Revard," " Le
Mont Rose," " Le Puy," " Tunisie," " La
Turbie," " Uriage-les-Bains," " Chemin de
fer du Midi : Pyrénées," " Chemin de fer
d'Orléans: Excursions en Auvergne" (1894),
" La Creuse et l'Indre," " Chemin de fer de
l'Ouest: Dieppe," " L'Auvergne (Orléans)."
Lefèvre (L.): " Nord. Eté a Cobourg,"
"Orléans Excursions aux Pyrénées," " Bains
de mer du Golfe de Gascogne," " Ouest
Excursions sur les côtes de Normandie, en
Bretagne, et à l'île de Jersey." Among other
designers for French railway companies and
watering-places may be named Orazi, whose
" Trouville " poster is reproduced on p. 181,
Balzer, Baylac, Japhet, and Ogé.

DESIGNS BY RÉALIER-DUMAS.

DESIGN BY ORAZI.

CHAPTER VI.

THE ARTISTIC POSTER IN ENG-
LAND: FROM FRED WALKER
TO DUDLEY HARDY.

WHILE the pictorial poster undoubtedly existed in England previous to the production of Fred Walker's "Woman in White," its artistic qualities were conspicuous by their absence. No body of artists who designed posters, such as that of which Gavarni was one in France, is to be met with in the history of English art until the present day. While, as Mr. Spielmann reminds us in a recent magazine article, Mr. Godfroy Durand and Mr. Walter Crane had both attempted the artistic *affiche* previous to Walker, the efforts of neither made a pronounced impression, nor were they productive of permanent results. The work of the first of these three artists announced the appearance of the then newly-founded "Graphic," and that of Mr. Walter Crane proclaimed the merits of a brand of lead pencils. It is interesting, as an example of Mr. Crane's immense versatility in decorative design, that he should be among the pioneers of the poster movement in this country. (That his early effort was overshadowed by Walker's very imposing work is not a matter of surprise. From the first, Walker appears to have been deeply impressed by the possibilities of the hoardings as a free art gallery. To use his own words, as quoted by (Mr. Spielmann): "I am impressed on doing all I can with a first attempt at what I consider might develop into a most important branch of art." How Walker's view has been realized the mere existence of this book is sufficient to prove. This design, which was done to advertise Wilkie Collins's novel, "The Woman in White," represents a magnificently-draped female figure stepping through a door out into the night. With one hand she opens the door, with the other she imposes silence on some person unseen. This was cut on wood by W. H. Hooper, who also engraved the small block we are permitted to reproduce here from "The Magazine of Art." (The design is in black and white, and has the limitations from the advertising point of view of black and white work; but, apart from this, it is in every way a work which could not fail to impress the passer-by. "The Woman in White" is, unfortunately, Walker's sole essay in the art of the poster; on the other hand, Mr. Walter Crane has produced a series which, we may hope, has yet to close. It would seem that over ten years elapsed between

his first and second attempts in the art of
the poster. We meet with him for the
second time in a design in blue and yellow

DESIGN BY FRED WALKER FOR "THE WOMAN IN WHITE."

which advertised the Covent Garden Pro-
menade Concerts given in 1880. This has
become extremely rare, and the artist him-

self does not, I believe, possess a copy.
Following the Covent Garden bill was one
announcing the performances in London of
the Paris Hippodrome Troupe. This is
merely an enlargement on a vast scale of a
classical drawing intended to adorn a book
describing the show, but it is distinctly interesting, more so, it seems to me, than the
pretty little coloured thing—a window-bill,
rather than a poster—which advertises
Hau's champagnes. Other posters by Mr.
Crane deal with an exhibition of his own
works, with various insurance companies,
with the " English Illustrated Magazine "
(an enlarged version of the cover), and
the exhibitions of the Arts and Crafts
Society. It will be seen that Mr. Crane's
contribution to the art of the poster is a
very substantial one, and if his designs do
not always fulfil the sweet uses of advertisement, they are generally marked by fine
taste. It is a matter of common knowledge
that Professor Herkomer has left hardly
any art or craft untouched, and it therefore
goes without saying that he has left some
of them unadorned. To succeed as painter,
etcher, carver, musician, poet and play-
wright, lecturer, and actor is not given to
mere man. Professor Herkomer's posters
cannot, I think, be considered among his
more fortunate performances. That done
for " The Magazine of Art " does not lack a
certain feeling for composition : the weird

DESIGN BY WALTER CRANE.

DESIGN BY WALTER CRANE.

DESIGN BY PROFESSOR HERKOMER, R.A, FOR "THE MAGAZINE OF ART."

BY PROFESSOR HERKOMER, R.A., FROM THE FIRST SKETCH FOR
THE POSTER FOR "BLACK AND WHITE."

O

creature who told us that "Black and White" was coming seemed to me to lack both dignity and grace, and, moreover, to possess very few compensating qualities. Amongst other posters by Professor Herkomer is one for his own exhibition, and one for an exhibition of pictures recently held at Oxford.

It should be noted that while most of the mural decorations of Mr. Crane and Professor Herkomer are, strictly speaking, posters, in that they were designed for the hoardings and for the hoardings alone, a great many designs and pictures by eminent artists have been reproduced and posted contrary to the original intention of their designers. The most prominent of these is, of course, Sir John Millais' famous "Bubbles," on the reproduction of which enormous sums have been spent. The thing is pretty enough, but cannot compete as an advertisement with a really good poster properly so called. Of course the name of Sir John Millais was one to conjure with, and the success of the thing has been, doubtless, great. But it is not an experiment one cares to see frequently repeated. Messrs. Pears were more happily inspired in the commission which they gave to Mr. Stacy Marks to produce a *bonâ fide* poster. His "Monks Shaving," seems to be most excellently conceived, and, indeed, to be the most interesting of Messrs. Pears' gallery of illustrated advertisements. Art has certainly played a very prominent part in the battle of the soaps. Mr. G. D. Leslie used his gifts to insist on the merits of the Sunlight brand, while Mr. Burton Barber pleaded pictorially for the Lifebuoy brand. A curious bit of poster-making was the reproduction of a random sketch of a girl sitting on a champagne cork, by Mr. Linley Sambourne, which seems to meet us at every turning. Again, Mr. Harry Furniss's man who had used Pears' soap years back, "and since then had used no other," is an enlarged reproduction used for advertising purposes of a drawing in " Punch." On the other hand, the " Minerva," which Mr. Poynter designed for the Guardian Assurance Company, was actually devised for the purpose of a mural advertisement. It cannot be strictly called a poster, insomuch as it is never seen in the open air unless glazed. It is a classical design in several colours, and is of a very elaborate character. For the purpose of exhibition indoors, it is glazed and mounted on linen with rollers. Another contemporary English painter who has received very high official recognition and has done a poster is Sir James Linton, P.R.I. His subject was assuredly an attractive one, " Antony and Cleopatra," but it can hardly be maintained that, for an artist of so great repute, he has produced an especially memorable design. It is a lithograph in one

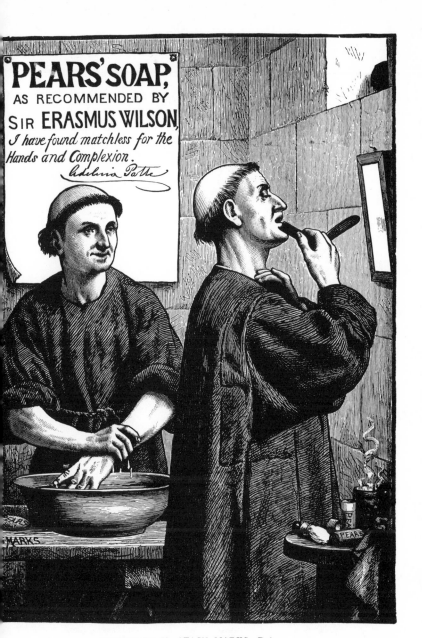

PEARS' SOAP,

AS RECOMMENDED BY

SIR ERASMUS WILSON,

I have found matchless for the Hands and Complexion.

Adelina Patti

MARKS

PEARS

DESIGN BY H. STACY MARKS, R.A.

HEAD OFFICE
11 LOMBARD STREET LONDON

FIRE   LIFE

GUARDIAN
Fire & Life
ASSURANCE
Company.

TOTAL
FVNDS
£ 4,342,000

ANNVAL
INCOME
£ 858,000

18 H 86

DESIGN BY EDWARD J. POYNTER, R.A.

colour, and measures fifty by fifty-two inches.
Its date is 1874, so it is clear that Sir James
Linton is among the little band who tried
to do something for the pictorial poster in

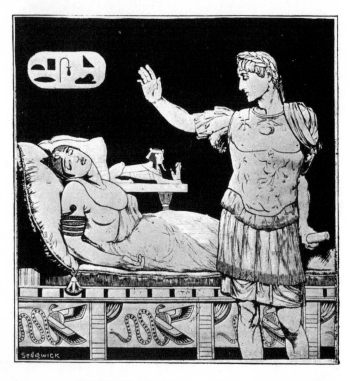

DESIGN BY SIR JAMES LINTON, P.R.I.

England when it was held of no account.
Mr. Charles Green, a member of the institution of which Sir James is president, produced a rather ingenious advertisement of
an exhibition of works in black and white
held some time ago in Mosley Street.   It

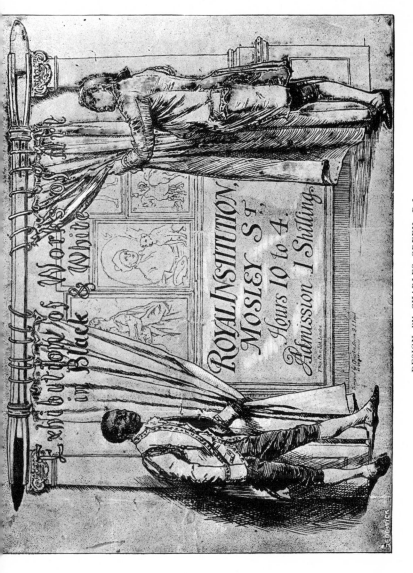

Exhibition of Works in Black & White

ROYAL INSTITUTION,
MOSLEY ST;
Hours 10 to 4.
Admission 1 Shilling.

DESIGN BY CHARLES GREEN, R.I.

PHILIP MORRIS
PATENT

A
LUXURY
TO THE
LIPS

PREVENTS
TONGUE
OR THROAT
IRRITATION

CORK
TIPPED
CIGARETTES
OF ALL LEADING TOBACCONISTS.

247

DESIGN BY LINLEY SAMBOURNE.

is not very large, and is a lithograph in one colour.

It will be observed that the artistic poster was in the air in England not very long after it began to develop in France. It does not, however, seem to have taken so great a hold on English artists or on the English public as on the artists and public of France. In England the artistic poster appears to have been received coldly or with indifference, and doubtless many designers who would have been glad to turn their attention to the poster were deterred therefrom by lack of public sympathy. But all this has happily been changed, and if the number of poster designers is to continue increasing at the present rate, the difficulty will be, not to find the artistic advertiser, but to find the thing to be advertised. A crowd of clever young men, actuated by the success which met the efforts of the designers dealt with in the next chapter, have rushed to the poster with results altogether important.

CHAPTER VII.

THE PICTORIAL POSTER IN ENGLAND: THE WORK OF DUDLEY HARDY, AUBREY BEARDSLEY, AND MAURICE GREIFFENHAGEN.

THE English artists of established reputation with whom I dealt in the last chapter, were, as we saw, so anxious to inform their posters with æsthetic qualities, that for the most part, they overlooked the obvious fact that their work was vain unless it really fulfilled its primary purpose of advertising. It was left for the three men (all of comparatively recent reputation) whose names head this chapter, to give the right direction; to insist that not art, but advertisement, was the first essential. It is not for an instant to be pretended that their achievement equals in importance that of the three designers discussed in a corresponding chapter in the section of this book devoted to France. Quantity of production, it is true, is a small matter in art; and yet, in so far as quantity of production entails experience, one is forced to take it into consideration.) The success of a man who has produced a hundred posters, or more, is scarcely to be expected of a designer, however ingenious, who is only making his first attempt. Moreover, to an artist accustomed to work on a small scale, it is a matter of extreme difficulty to appreciate, and when in the throes of production to keep in mind, the essentials of a design intended to be seen at a considerable distance in the open air. He is apt to be tempted into pretty detail or subtle and harmonious colour, and therefore to forget that he should be simple almost to the point of crudeness.) (Under these circumstances, it is not less remarkable than it is encouraging, that Mr. Hardy, Mr. Beardsley, and Mr. Greiffenhagen in their earliest essays apprehended the situation at once, and produced posters which inevitably caught the eye of the beholder and created an impression which remained with him for a considerable time.) Differing in all else, the first designs of these three artists were alike, in that they were admirable advertisements. From every hoarding in London, from the walls of every station on the Underground Railway, one was vehemently called upon to purchase a new weekly, or a new series of an old one, or to visit the Avenue Theatre. If the call was resisted, it was assuredly no fault of these artist-advertisers. To suggest that what they have done would have been impossible,

DESIGN BY DUDLEY HARDY (FOR "TO-DAY").

DESIGN BY DUDLEY HARDY (FOR "A GAIETY GIRL").

or at least improbable, if France had nòt paved the way, is scarcely to discount their immediate and unequivocal success: even the greatest artist is unwise if he does not condescend to make use of the work of the past.

It is, I think, Mr. Dudley Hardy who, of the three artists named, owes most to France. He has made a variation, a very personal and alluring variation, be it said, of a theme essentially Gallic in its unrestrained gaiety, its reckless joyousness. There is something of Chéret, and there is even more of Jan Van Beers, in the end-of-the-century girl, elegant as she is impudent, whom Mr. Hardy depicts with such amazing *verve* and *abandon*. She is too light-hearted, too irresponsible, to be a daughter of this land of grey and rainy skies; she takes nothing seriously, save perchance a detail of her costume. And yet she is stamped with Mr. Hardy's personality as thoroughly as are the charming *parisiennes* of Chéret with the individuality of their inventor. Mr. Hardy began, and began wisely, by trusting for his effect to a single bold figure. Elaborate composition implies detail, and detail is one of the pitfalls of the designer of posters. Take, for example, the vast sheets which were employed to advertise one of the spectacles at Olympia. The overcrowding of small figures and closely-realized views either

P

produced no impression whatsoever on the spectator, or at the most an impression due entirely to the immensity of the sheets. Mr. Hardy's series of posters commenced most auspiciously with that audacious young lady in a yellow dress, saucy hat, and flying black boa, who, not deigning to entreat, compelled the passer-by to rush to the nearest bookstall for a copy of Mr. Jerome's weekly " To-Day." Later, in similar vein, came the dashing girl in red, used by the manager of the Prince of Wales's Theatre to insist on the merits of " A Gaiety Girl." It may be doubted whether any more effective mural advertisement has ever been seen in London than that formed by half-a-dozen copies of this poster, arranged in the manner of a frieze in front of the theatre during the run of the piece. If the idea was that of the bill-sticker, the man was a genius of his kind : I cannot help suspecting, however, that the striking arrangement was due to Mr. Hardy himself. Or perhaps it was the happy thought of an outsider. In addition to the large " Gaiety Girl " poster, the two smaller bills which this artist designed to advertise the same play, full as they were of dash and go, must not be overlooked. To the collector they have a merit which he will not fail to appreciate. They are of manageable size, and this is more than can be said of most of Mr. Hardy's productions.

It must not be thought, however, that

DESIGN BY DUDLEY HARDY (FROM SKETCH).

Mr. Hardy can do no more than repeat with slight variety of detail the *chic* girl to whom he first introduced us ; already, notwithstanding the comparatively small number of his designs, he has shown a very commendable versatility. The proprietors of " St. Paul's," in the days when that journal regaled its readers on the portraits, not of dancing girls, but of right reverend prelates, commissioned Mr. Hardy for a large design appropriate to the semi-ecclesiastical character of their journal. The choice, in view of the " Yellow Girl," was a somewhat curious one ; but the experiment justified itself. The artist rose to the occasion ; on the hoardings of London there appeared a woman of austere, even saintly, demeanour, clad in sombre robes, and armed with a spike of the Madonna lily. In spite of the low scheme of colour, the design was very telling as an advertisement. It has become very rare ; indeed, notwithstanding the fact that the dealers quote it at various prices in their catalogues, it may be questioned whether it is to be procured at all. When the policy of " St. Paul's " was changed — when it stepped down from its shrine to join the multitude and be of the world, worldly— the art of Mr. Hardy was once more called in to introduce the paper in its new guise. For the first time, so far as I know, he attempted composition. His idea was a happy one. The poster represented a young lady, evidently light-hearted and of unquestionably fantastic costume, see-sawing on a quarter of the moon with a gentleman of slight intellect, but exceedingly smart clothes.   Seen under certain conditions the composition is distinctly effective, but from a long distance it fails to assert itself as do Mr. Hardy's simpler designs.   In his most recent effort he has returned to the single figure, and he has done nothing more striking than his bill for " The Chieftain," at the Savoy Theatre, which represents a man in picturesque costume on a red ground.   The lettering of nearly all Mr. Hardy's posters is admirable. It is invented by the artist himself, and forms an essential part of the design.   For the rest, it should be remembered that the poster is a mere incident in Mr. Hardy's art career. As an illustrator he is with us everywhere ; as a painter he is held in deserved esteem. It is to be hoped, for the sake of the artistic poster in England, that he will continue to devote some of his time to a branch of art in which, in comparatively a short time, he has so greatly succeeded.

The art of Mr. Aubrey Beardsley has been so enthusiastically received, on the one hand, as a new revelation, and so passionately condemned, on the other, as the mere glorification of a hideous and putrescent aspect of modern life, that it is difficult to consider his work with calmness.   One thing, however, is certain : an impression

DESIGN BY DUDLEY HARDY.

DESIGN BY DUDLEY HARDY.

of some kind, whether agreeable or the re-
verse, it has undoubtedly left upon all who
have seen it. It cannot be dismissed by
stating that it is derivative rather than
original; that to a large extent it is the outcome of Japan, and in a less degree of the
old English school of caricaturists. Whether
it be good or bad, the extraordinary impression it has made cannot be gainsaid. It is
probable that the work of no young designer
of recent times has called forth so much
homage of imitation, so great an amount of
that kind of caricature which is among the
sincerest forms of flattery. Mr. Beardsley's
eccentricities are so pronounced, that to
parody his work was simply to do the
obvious. From " Punch," august by reason of its fifty years of tradition, to the
poorest comic rag produced to catch the
errand-boy's spare halfpenny, is a far cry;
and yet the former, no less than the latter,
has treated its readers to a series of pictorial
Beardsleyisms. It would have been wonderful, indeed, if Mr. Beardsley, who is
nothing if not modern, had not attempted
the artistic poster. His opportunity came
when the Avenue Theatre was taken by an
enthusiastic and courageous young actress
for the production of plays by living English
writers, which, whatever their fate from the
commercial point of view, were at least to
possess definite merits as pieces of literature. In order to advertise Dr. Todhunter's

"Comedy of Sighs," and Mr. G. Bernard Shaw's "Arms and the Man," Mr. Beardsley excelled himself, and designed perhaps the most remarkable poster ever seen, up to that time, in London.

Nothing so compelling, so irresistible, had ever been posted on the hoardings of the metropolis before. Some gazed at it with awe, as if it were the final achievement of modern art ; others jeered at it as a palpable piece of buffoonery : everybody, however, from the labourer hurrying in the dim light of the morning to his work, to the prosperous stockbroker on his way to the " House," was forced to stop and look at it. Hence, it fulfilled its primary purpose to admiration ; it was a most excellent advertisement. The old theatrical poster represented, in glaring colours, the hero in a supreme moment of exaltation, or the heroine in the depths of despair. Mr. Beardsley did not condescend to illustrate, but produced a design, irrelevant and tantalizing to the average man, though doubtless full of significance to himself. In many respects the Avenue bill must be considered the best poster which so far has come from this artist's hands. The very graceful figure on a small poster for " The Yellow Book " speaks for itself. It is more vivid, more curious, than either of the two done for a London publisher. Most collectors, however, will treasure even more highly

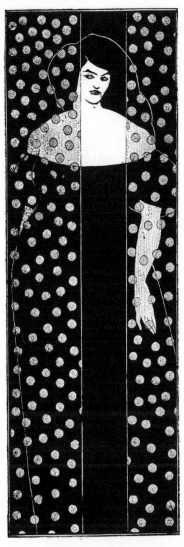

DESIGN BY AUBREY BEARDSLEY (FOR THE AVENUE THEATRE).

DESIGN BY AUBREY BEARDSLEY (FOR "THE YELLOW BOOK ").

the charming design done by Mr. Beardsley
to advertise the Pseudonym series of short
stories.   In it we meet with the artist in
his less mordant mood.   The sketch of the

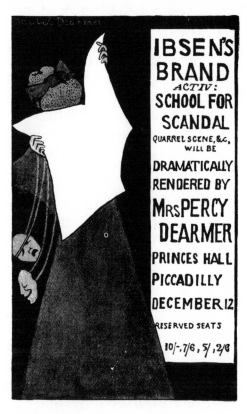

DESIGN BY MABEL DEARMER.

old bookshop in the background is quite
delightful, and the whole design is less grotesque than most of Mr. Beardsley's productions.   The arrangement in purple and

white, which he did for the same firm, is a very striking performance in his later manner. [Its importance as a poster is, however, seriously discounted by the fact that the design has nothing whatsoever to do with the text, which has been added in a manner almost inconceivably clumsy.]

The success of Mr. Beardsley in the production of artistic posters has encouraged a host of imitators, so that it is quite within the bounds of possibility that he will found something in the nature of a school. Already, on the other side of the Atlantic, more than one artist has been inspired by him. The posters of Mr. Bradley, for example, with which I shall deal later, are unquestionably adaptations, at once skilful and intelligent, of Mr. Beardsley's decorative manner. Again, to return to England, the pleasant arrangement in red and white, designed by Mrs. Dearmer to advertise a recital recently given by her in London, proves that she has been affected by the simplicity and directness which are so conspicuous among the merits of Mr. Beardsley in his essays in the art of the hoarding. Of his many parodists only one, I think, has actually attempted the poster. The essay in question was made by Mr. J. Hearn, under the signature of "Weirdsly Daubery," and the result was very fantastic and amusing. The design was done for some amateur theatricals at Oxford, and it was curious to

DESIGN BY J. HEARN (WEIRDSLY DAUBERY).

DESIGN BY MAURICE GRIEFFENHAGEN.

meet this atom of the so-called decadence flaunting itself, with strange incongruity, in every nook and corner of " the sweet city of the dreaming spires."

The case of Mr. Maurice Grieffenhagen is similar to that of Mr. Dudley Hardy, insomuch as both have been well known for some time to the public as painters and as the producers of very accomplished work in black and white. At present Mr. Grieffenhagen, as a designer of posters, can only be judged by a single production. It may be said at once that nothing more distinguished, nothing which is less imitative or derivative, has come from English hands than Mr. Grieffenhagen's advertisement for the " Pall Mall Budget." Admirable alike in colour and in pattern, the poster is entirely appropriate to its purpose of keeping before the eyes of the public a publication which escaped frivolity on the one hand and dulness on the other. All who watch the development of the artistic poster in England with interest, cannot but hope that the " Pall Mall Budget " poster will be the first of a series by the same artist equally delightful and original.

It is interesting to note that while we are still a long way behind the French in the matter of the artistic poster, the productions of the three artists with whom I have just dealt have received a cordial welcome at the hands of Parisian collectors. In the dealers' shops you may see Mr. Hardy's "Gaiety Girl" side by side with Lautrec's "Reine de Joie," while Mr. Grieffenhagen's young lady in red looks with demure surprise at the antics of her more frivolous sisters, as depicted by Jules Chéret. There is, again, a steady demand for anything by Mr. Beardsley, who, it would seem, has already become an established favourite with French connoisseurs. As we shall see in another chapter, the prices put in Paris upon English posters compare very favourably with those at which the works of the ablest French designers are valued. In matters of art, few cities are more insular and intolerant than the French metropolis; and those English artists who are devoting themselves to the poster, should be encouraged by enthusiastic recognition where enthusiasm was least to be expected.

CHAPTER VIII.

THE WORK OF OTHER CONTEM-
PORARY ENGLISH DESIGNERS.

SINCE this book was commenced as the com-
panion, rather than the rival, of that of M.
Maindron, English designers of the poster
have multiplied in a degree altogether phe-
nomenal.

(Up to the time in question, as we have
already seen, the English artist who attempted the poster was exceptional.) The
famine, which was prevalent only a year or
two ago, has become the abundance of to-
day, so that where one expected a dearth of
subject matter, one has in fact an excess.
It seems to me that, apart from the English
pioneers, whom we have already considered,
the brothers Beggarstaff, in reality Messrs.
Pryde and Simpson, two young artists, are
entitled to the first place among the makers
of the English artistic poster. They have
best appreciated the essence of their business : less than almost any native designers,
they are innocent of any homage of imitation. They have imitated neither Chéret
nor Lautrec : it may well be that they have

had the wisdom to take a hint here and there from both of these masters of the art of the *affiche*. As yet the hoardings of London are screaming with the vulgar designs of the advertiser's hack. The admirable art of the Beggarstaffs is, up to now, infrequently met with. Their curious advertisement for Sir Henry Irving's production of " Becket," was eclipsed by that done for the same manager's " Don Quixote," while the latter has to give place to one intended to announce a special issue of " Harper's Magazine." All of these force themselves on the collector's attention. They are at once striking and artistic; they cry their wares well, and they are a delight to the eyes. The lettering in the Harper poster is beyond all praise. Of its kind, it is the most beautiful English lettering of which I know. At the Aquarium Exhibition the Beggarstaff's showed four posters which advertised Nobody's Blue, Nobody's Candles, Nobody's Niggers, and Nobody's Pianos. If each " Nobody " is not rapidly converted into " Somebody," the various manufacturers and proprietors of the articles mentioned above must be very stupid people. All were excellent ; that which advertised Nobody's Pianos was a most curious and a most original performance. It seems to me that the Beggarstaffs have few serious rivals in England, and not very many in France. Their works should help very

DESIGN BY THE BROTHERS BEGGARSTAFF.

considerably in the task of revolutioniz-
ing the English pictorial poster. The

6^D THE
HOUR
ILLUSTRATED

impression created by
their designs on French-
men, who are past mas-
ters in the art of the
hoarding, is most favour-
able.

It will be remembered
that when Mr. Sickert
took it into his head to
depict the Sisters Lloyd
in their music-hall
habit, the critics fell out
greatly. Even the young
ladies in question had,
it is said, scant affection
for a design in which
everything was sugges-
ted and nothing declared.
They had, it is true, the
recompense of advertise-

DESIGN BY THE BROTHERS
BEGGARSTAFF.

ment, and that, to a music-hall singer, is a
very sweet recompense. It was characteristic

of Mr. Sickert that he should go to the music-
halls for a subject.   The " New English
Art Club " is devoted to things which are

DESIGN BY THE BROTHERS BEGGARSTAFF.

new and strange, the artistic poster amongst
them.   Mr. Sickert is not the only one of
the members of this club who have made an
essay in the latest form of applied art.   Mr.
Beardsley, Mr. R. Anning Bell, and Mr.

DESIGN BY THE BROTHERS BEGGARSTAFF.

HAMLET

DESIGN BY THE BROTHERS BEGGARSTAFF.

DESIGN BY THE BROTHERS BEGGARSTAFF.

Wilson Steer are amongst those of his col-
leagues who have done the same thing. Mr.
Sickert's poster, which is, I believe, as yet
unpublished, is in four colours. It is calculated to make a good advertisement, and
one can only hope soon to meet with it on
the hoardings. As an impressionist painter
of talent, Mr. Wilson Steer is as well known
as Mr. Sickert. A "New English Art Club"
Exhibition without his work would be one
which lacked a most characteristic feature.
Mr. Steer gave us an opportunity of appre-
ciating his talent as a painter by organiz-
ing a show of his own work. To advertise
this he did a poster, which was excellent of
its kind, and is in consequence very rare.
It is a comparatively small lithograph in
four colours, and is quite unlike this artist's
other work. It leans, it seems to me,
towards Pre-Raphaelitism rather than towards Impressionism. An artist who has
certainly sat at the feet of Mr. Whistler is
Mr. Mortimer Menpes. To advertise several
exhibitions of his paintings, he has invented
at least three posters, which certainly do not
lack the merit of originality. He has ab-
stained from the frivolous girl and grotesque
man. The "France," the "Venice," and the
"India" are in their way considerable
achievements in dainty design and quiet
and harmonious colour. Mr. Menpes, by
being intentionally simple, has arrived at
notable conspicuity. All this artist's de-

signs are of small size, and are appropriate
rather to the notice board than to the
hoarding. Nothing more opposite to the
fastidious productions of Mr. Menpes could
be conceived than the vigorous poster by
Mr. Lockhart Bogle advertising a Scottish
Athletic Gathering, held in 1892. This
is a large lithograph, consisting of a single
figure of a Highlander, which, if not remarkably beautiful, is drawn with vigour
and with no small accuracy. Mr. Brangwyn
is one of those English painters of whom
we are entitled to be proud. His directness, the audacity of his impressionism, the
splendour (if sometimes ill-considered) of
his colour schemes, cannot be passed over
even by those who have slight sympathy
with his method. That, if so inclined, he
would produce a poster at once startling and
artistic is not to be denied. The one which
he has already designed to advertise an exhibition of South African pictures by himself and Mr. William Hunt, held at the
Japanese Gallery, is certainly by no means
worthy his remarkable talent, and one trusts
that he will cease for a moment from painting pictures and produce a poster which
shall be memorable in the history of the
affiche in England.

Mr. Frank Richards is nothing if not
versatile; his exhibition, held recently at
the Dowdeswells' Galleries, came as a surprise to all who were unacquainted with his

Within the poster image:

THE GOUPIL GALLERY
5 REGENT
STREET PALL
MALL.
EXHIBITION OF
PAINTINGS
BY P. WILSON
STEER.
ADMISSION
1 SHILLING
10 TO 6

SEDGWICK

DESIGN BY P. WILSON STEER.

DESIGN BY LEWIS BAUMER.

PICK-ME-UP

DESIGN BY L. RAVEN-HILL.

clever painting. In this exhibition his
pictures ranged from a large study of Mr.
Clive as "Hamlet" to slight but beautiful
studies of Venice under various atmospheric
conditions. In his poster work, of which at
present little has been seen, Mr. Richards
shows that, to some extent, he is under the influence of Mr. Dudley Hardy. Mr. Richards,
no less than Mr. Hardy, is undeniably up
to date, and his work is really effective.
Among the most recent additions to the
ranks of our popular illustrators is Mr. Lewis
Baumer. One meets with his work everywhere; in "To-Day" and in the short-
lived "Unicorn." His bills to advertise
the Academy students' annual burlesque
are pretty, if they are nothing else. Mr.
Baumer has certainly still to make his mark
as a poster designer. The Artistic Supply
Company, who are paying special attention
to the pictorial poster, have already produced
a dainty little *affiche* by him. It may be
noted here that the company in question
have arranged with some of the most eminent English designers for the reproduction
of artistic posters, and that several, which
illustrate these pages, do so only on account
of their permission most generously given.

Among other services which the comic
journal "Pick-Me-Up" has rendered to the
artistic public is the extremely important
one of emphasizing, and giving a congenial
outlet to, the remarkable talent of Mr.

DESIGN BY L. RAVEN-HILL.

DESIGN BY SYDNEY ADAMSON.

Raven-Hill. From almost the first, his connection with the journal in question has been a very intimate one. Hardly a number is without a specimen of his powerful drawing and his gift of comic invention. While suggesting, in the best sense, the style of the incomparable Charles Keene, Mr. Raven-Hill's work in black and white is the outcome of his own personality. It would have been strange if this very modern artist had not produced pictorial posters : his talent was perfectly adapted to his doing so with success. His small bills for " Pick-Me-Up " are vigorous in drawing, bold in colour, and of a pleasant fantasy. They only measure twenty by thirty inches, but they are very telling. A complete set of them is a most desirable addition to the collector's portfolio. Another accomplished member of the staff of "Pick-Me-Up," Mr. Edgar Wilson, has designed a bill for the recently defunct journal, " The Unicorn." It is effective, but to me personally, the colour scheme is even more crude than the exigencies of a poster demand. Mr. Reginald Cleaver, whose sketches of scenes in the House of Commons created so favourable an impression in " The Daily Graphic," has not yet, I believe, deliberately produced a pictorial poster ; but one of his drawings, reproduced on a large scale, lends itself well enough to the purposes of mural advertisement. Mr. Sydney Adamson, the art editor of

" To-day " and " The Idler," has done a
bill which, when it is seen, will be held, I
have small doubt, a very striking performance.   It is happily conceived and boldly
executed, and should make a striking patch
of colour on the hoardings.

Merely to chronicle the names of the innumerable Wilsons who are producing pictures
would take quite a considerable space.   It
may be noted in passing that, like Edgar of
that name, Mr. W. Wilson has also attempted
an *affiche*.

Among others who have designed posters
which have yet to be seen on the hoardings
are Mr. Max Cowper, Mr. A. R. Miller, Mr.
Kerr Lawson, Mr. F. H. Townsend, whose
black and white work one meets everywhere,
Mr. Roche, a prominent member of the
Glasgow School, and one of the greatest
living English artists, Mr. Phil May.

Mr. Phil May is not the only " Punch "
man who has been seized with the prevail-
ing mania for the production of posters.
His colleague, Mr. Bernard Partridge, has
already designed one which is reproduced
in these pages.   One associates Mr. Partridge with dainty and idyllic work rather than
with work which is vigorous, but his first
essay in the poster seems to me to be very
promising.   Mr. J. T. Manuel's work is as
unlike that of Mr. Bernard Partridge as
possible.   His pictures might be by a clever
member of the young French School who

DESIGN BY MAX COWPER.

DESIGN BY A. R. MILLAR.

S

DESIGN BY KERR LAWSON.

DESIGN BY BERNARD PARTRIDGE.

DESIGN BY CHARLES FFOULKES.

DESIGN BY CHARLES FFOULKES.

DESIGN BY LÉON SOLON.

DESIGN BY A. MORROW.

DESIGN BY A. MORROW.

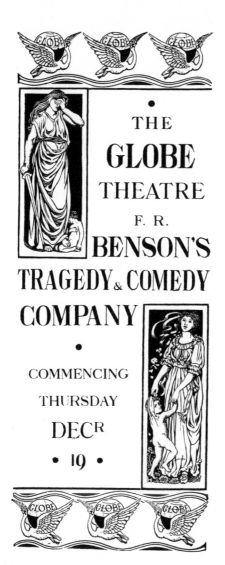

THE
GLOBE
THEATRE
F. R.
BENSON'S
TRAGEDY & COMEDY
COMPANY

•

COMMENCING

THURSDAY

DEC^R

• 19 •

DESIGN BY HEYWOOD SUMNER.

T

THE
GLOBE THEATRE

Sole Lessee · · · · F. R. BENSON.

F. R. BENSON'S

Shakesperian Company in
A MIDSUMMER NIGHT'S
DREAM ✳ *on* THURSDAY,
Dec. **19**, *and every ensuing*
evening until further notice

DESIGN BY HEYWOOD SUMNER.

have taken more than a hint from Forain.
The designs for posters which Mr. Manuel
exhibited at the Westminster Aquarium, if
not so distinctive of his talent as his contri-
butions in black and white to " Pick-Me-
Up," were not without definite merit. Of
the three, that catalogued as " A Music-hall
Singer" struck me as the best. It should
be purchased by Miss Minnie Cunningham,
for the likeness between her, and the young
lady it represents, if accidental, is marvel-
lous. Among young decorative painters of
the day who are not mere imitators of such
masters as Sir Edward Burne-Jones or
Puvis de Chavannes, but have invented a
style for themselves, must be included Mr.
Charles Ffoulkes. The two examples of
his poster-work here reproduced are as
beautiful in colour as they are refined in
pattern. Moreover, they proclaim themselves in loud tones. Their tones, however,
are those of a silver trumpet rather than
those of cymbal or of gong. At times Mr.
Ffoulkes forsakes his lofty imaginings and
depicts *chic* young ladies quite in the best
French manner. Mr. L. Solon's poster,
reproduced here, is a very characteristic
example of his decorative style. In invent-
ing it, the artist has clearly kept before him
the fact that a poster cannot live by beauty
alone ; if, happily, there be beauty, there
must of necessity be advertisement, else is
failure inevitable.

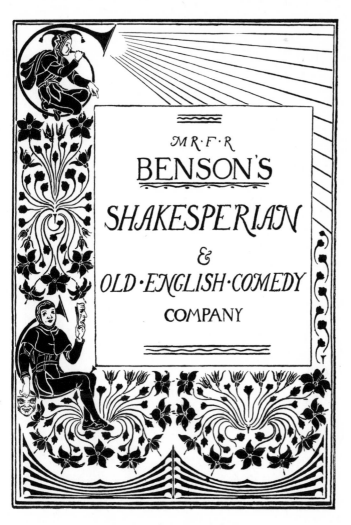

MR·F·R
BENSON'S
SHAKESPERIAN
&
OLD·ENGLISH·COMEDY
COMPANY

DESIGN BY HEYWOOD SUMNER.

Very unlike Mr. Solon's poster are the *affiches* of Mr. Heywood Sumner; those which I reproduce here seem to me to be very characteristic of his graceful gift of design. Mr. Morrow is already an established favourite on the hoardings of London, and justly so in that his performances are of exceptional merit. His "Illustrated Bits"

DESIGN BY SIDNEY HAWARD.

is a radiant affair, and his "New Woman" makes quite a pretty picture. His works should certainly be collected.

Of Mr. R. Anning Bell it is not too much to say that for versatility only Mr. Walter Crane among English artists can be said to rival him, and, what is far more important, his success in a medley of mediums is not to be gainsaid.   His poster for the Liverpool School of Art, over which he presides, is a magnificent piece of decoration, and nothing so fine, in its way, has ever been seen on English hoardings.   It takes one up to the Elgin marbles ; it is an oasis of the classical in a desert of the new.   I can only mention the following native artists, not previously considered, who have produced pictorial posters of interest : Mr. F. Barnard ("Everybody should read in the European School"), Mr. F. Simpson ("Land of the Midnight Sun," "To Norway Fjords"), Mr. Robert Fowler, R.I., whose poster for the Walker Art Gallery is here illustrated, Mr. Sidney Haward (p. 279), Mr. Skipworth ("An Artist's Model"), Mr. Skinner ("Pall Mall Magazine"), Mr. Starr Wood and Mr. A. G. Draper.

I have already remarked that the poster movement in this country amounts to a positive revolution.   No young artist is satisfied unless he has a hand in the decoration of the hoardings; the gold frame is for the time forgotten, and all have their eyes on the lithographer's stone.   France has undoubtedly had a long start of us, but if she is to retain her supremacy she must look to her laurels.   Our young men are beating at her doors, though beating only in a spirit of friendly rivalry.   Happily, between England and France there is, at this moment, only one war—the war of the pictorial poster.

DESIGN BY ROBERT FOWLER, R.I.

CITY OF LIVERPOOL SCHOOL OF ARCHITECTURE AND APPLIED ART

CLASSES IN ARCHITECTURE MODELLING PAINTING AND DRAWING CARVING IN WOOD AND STONE ORNAMENTAL WROUGHT IRON WORK ETC. ETC. FOR PARTICULARS APPLY TO THE DIRECTOR

UNIVERSITY COLLEGE

DESIGN BY R. ANNING BELL.

CHAPTER IX.

THE PICTORIAL POSTER IN AMERICA.

IN the sweet uses of advertisement the American is surely an expert, and it would have been curious indeed, if he had over-looked so obvious and so effective a method of advertising as the pictorial poster. Finding, in the notorious phrase of Mr. Whistler, that "Art was on the town," the American advertiser was one of the most eager of those passing gallants who chucked her under the chin. Who it was originated the artistic poster movement in the States, it were hard to say with certainty: it may have been Mr. Matt. Morgan. Among recent American poster producers, three, however, are most con-spicuous, Mr. Edward Penfield, Mr. Louis J. Rhead, and Mr. Will. H. Bradley. It is probable that the first-named was the inno-vator: at least, one would be tempted to judge so from the quantity of his designs.

Mr. Penfield is still young, having been born at Brooklyn in the year 1866, so that if he was the first American artist to deal with the poster, the movement in that continent is obviously a recent one. Most of his posters are on a small scale, and partake of the nature of window-bills rather than of placards especially destined to the hoarding. At the same time, Mr. Penfield has been by no means slow to appreciate that it is the first

DESIGN BY EDWARD PENFIELD.

business of an advertisement to advertise, and his appreciation of this fact, coupled with a very dainty fancy and no small technical skill, has led to results which are of unquestionable importance. With his earliest efforts I cannot pretend to be well acquainted. In 1893 he produced for a firm at Salem a large bill which measures eighty-one by forty-two inches. The subject is a girl in a black dress and yellow jacket who is laden with packages. For

DESIGN BY EDWARD PENFIELD.

the publications of the firm of Harpers, Mr. Penfield has done quite a quantity of excellent and artistic advertisements. Amongst the most effective is one produced for a special midsummer number of

"Harper's Bazar," representing a girl playing a banjo, divided by a crimson sun from an attentive listener of the opposite sex. Again, for the issue of July, 1894, the artist gives us a girl in white lighting red crackers arranged to spell the name of the month. For the February number of the following year, we are presented, most appropriately, with a gentleman posting a valentine in an orange coloured letter-box. In April of the same year, Mr. Penfield gives us Joan of Arc in yellow, wielding sword and staff. Amongst the numerous books which Mr. Penfield has advertised may be mentioned "The Cloister and the Hearth," "Pastime Stories," "Our English Cousins," and "Perlycross." This artist's work is always ingeniously conceived, and the colour schemes are not seldom pleasantly audacious. Mr. Penfield gives us very agreeable versions of the American girl in general, and of the "summer girl" in particular. His maidens are adorably conscious of their power to charm, and are fully alive to the fact that their gowns are of the smartest.

To turn from Mr. Penfield to Mr. Louis J. Rhead is to turn to an artist settled in the United States, but English by birth and education. Mr. Rhead was born at Etruria, that unclassical place with the classical name, and comes of a family of artists. He was, I believe, a student at South Ken-

DESIGN BY EDWARD PENFIELD.

U

DESIGN BY LOUIS J. RHEAD (FOR THE NEW YORK "SUN").

sington for several years, and only reached
America in 1883.   He has exhibited at the

The Modern Cleanser

Millions now use Pearline

DESIGN BY LOUIS J. RHEAD.

Salon and the Academy and other important picture shows.

Mr. Rhead seems to have taken to the

poster with the greatest enthusiasm, and he
has undoubtedly produced a series of curious
and striking designs.   By far the most important of his efforts, though not the largest,
are the designs which he has done for the
New York "Sun."   In one of these very
daring productions, a crimson sun glows in
a golden sky.   The ground is green, the
footpath and the trees are blue, while the
girl's costume is garnet and red.   It must
be confessed that this colour scheme sounds
somewhat formidable, but Mr. Rhead has
invented an arrangement at once artistic
and compelling.   The lettering, it must be
noted with regret, is not from his own
hand.   One of the largest of Mr. Rhead's
posters is the " Pearline," in which a girl in
a green and red dress is represented in the
act of pinning a sheet on to a line.   This
design measures forty-one by twenty-eight
inches.   Of considerable size, and of no
small merit, is the poster executed for the
" Century," Christmas, 1894, the chief
feature of which is a girl with a peacock.
Among other effective designs which stand
to the credit of Mr. Rhead may be mentioned those advertising " Harper's Bazar,"
Christmas, 1890, Thanksgiving, 1894, and
Christmas of the same year.   For the
" Century," besides that already noticed, he
has done several interesting posters, and he
helped to advertise various numbers of " St.
Nicholas " last year.   It is to be noted that

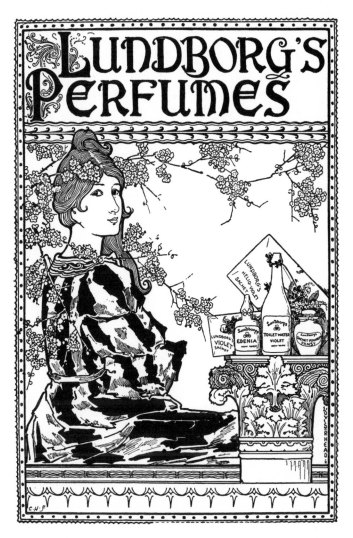

DESIGN BY LOUIS J. RHEAD.

Mr. Louis Rhead has held an exhibition of his posters, the catalogue of which, by reason of its very characteristic and per-

DESIGN BY LOUIS J. RHEAD.

sonal decorations, is highly esteemed by collectors of those unconsidered trifles which end in becoming especially dear to the connoisseur.

Among the magazines of the world, the "Chap Book," which emanates from Chicago, is by no means the least interesting. Fascinating as is the title, the contents of this little periodical are still more so; its editors seem to have eschewed banality, and to have gone in for novelty, even when the new did not possess an extraordinary degree of merit. It were meet that so original a publication should have an advertiser of corresponding eccentricity. In Mr. Will. H. Bradley, the proprietors of the "Chap Book" undoubtedly possess such an one. Born at Springfield, Massachusetts, Mr. Bradley lives in Chicago, and to that town and its publications he has mainly devoted his energies as an artist advertiser. It will hardly be disputed that he has seen and assimilated, in no small degree, the manner of Mr. Aubrey Beardsley. He is, however, a great deal more than a mere imitator; what he has borrowed, he has borrowed with conspicuous intelligence, and nobody could for a moment accuse him of anything approaching petty larceny. Among his most important posters is a colossal one which, in the manner of Mr. Beardsley, proclaims the attractions of the drama by Mr. Henry Arthur Jones, entitled "The Masqueraders." In 1894 Mr. Bradley advertised the "Chap Book" by means of two dancers in red and brown costumes; the following year he insisted on the same

publication by means of a girl in white and
a.man in black ; and yet again, through the
medium of a young lady in blue, mixed up
with trees in intense purple, outlined with
red and white ; and several other equally
effective compositions.

Mr. Bradley is, however, not the only
artist intimately connected with Chicago
who has distinguished himself in the production of posters. A native of that city,
Mr. Will. Carqueville, has done very interesting work for the firm of Lippincott's.
In the year 1894, at least one design by him
was commissioned, and in the succeeding
year he produced four or more. That he
is not afraid of colour is proved by the fact
that in the poster done for Lippincott's,
March, 1895, he combines dark purple,
yellow, blue, and bronze. In another design
we meet with red, purple, yellow, and blue.
Mr. Kenyon Cox is an American artist
whose fame is by no means confined to the
United States. A pupil of Gerôme and
Carolus Duran, he has, so far as I know,
made only one essay in the art of the
poster. This measures eighty-one by forty
inches, and is in black and white. It represents a male figure carrying a torch, and is
an advertisement for "Scribner's Magazine."
Mr. Scotson Clark was a schoolfellow of
Mr. Aubrey Beardsley. He has, among
other posters, done two to which the picturesque labels of " Our Lady of the Peacock

Feather," and "Lady of the Iris," are attached.
In addition, for the March issue of the
" Bookman," 1895, Mr. Scotson Clark drew
a monk, with book in hand.   Mr. George
Wharton Edwards, the well-known painter
in water-colours, must be credited with three
designs for the " Century," in the months
of February, March, and April, 1895. Moreover, by means of a drawing of a girl and a
peacock, he proclaimed the twenty-eighth
annual exhibition of the American Water-
Colour Society, in addition to designing a
bill for a book entitled " The Man Who
Married the Moon." The advertising enterprise of the firm of Scribner has made
poster-collectors the richer by one or two
productions by Mr. Charles Gibson Dana.
He it was who announced, with no inconsiderable skill, the issues of " Scribner's
Magazine" for the months of January and
February, 1895.   Mr. Archie Gunn is the
son of a well-known drawing master in one
of the large towns of the Midlands. Leaving
England for America, he found an outlet
for his talent as a draughtsman on the New
York journal " Truth."   His work is nearly
always vivacious, even where it is not par-
ticularly original.   His posters were done
for the " Illustrated American," and are by
no means bad examples of his craftsman-
ship. Like most prominent American artists,
Mr. Thomas Burford Meteyard studied in
Paris. His poster to advertise a book called

DESIGN BY WILL H. BRADLEY.

DESIGN BY WILL. H. BRADLEY.

DESIGN BY WILL. H. BRADLEY.

X

A FRAGMENT OF A DESIGN BY WILL. H. BRADLEY.

DESIGN BY WILL. H. BRADLEY.

A FRAGMENT OF A POSTER FOR "THE MASQUERADERS," BY
WILL. H. BRADLEY.

DESIGN BY WILL. H. BRADLEY.

THE QVEST OF THE HOLY GRAIL

EDWIN A ABBEY

PUBLISHED BY R·H·RUSSELL & SON NEW YORK

DESIGN BY E. A. ABBEY (FOR A BOOK PUBLISHED IN NEW YORK BY
MESSRS. R. H. RUSSELL, AND IN ENGLAND BY THE FINE ART SOCIETY).

" Songs from Vagabondia " is in black and white, and consists of portraits of the artist himself and the authors of the book, Mr. Bliss Carman and Mr. Richard Hovey. A limited number of copies were printed " sur Japon," and these, I believe, are rare. As in the case of so many other American artists, Mr. Francis Day's poster work was done for the most part for the great illustrated magazines which do such credit to the United States, as an art-producing nation. Mr. Day's design for " St. Nicholas," Christmas, 1894, seems to me altogether agreeable, while in the series designed for "Scribner's Magazine," more than one interesting thing will be found.

In dealing with the poster in England, we have noticed the fact that one woman, Mrs. Dearmer, has succeeded in producing a bill at once artistic and effective. Miss Ethel Reed would seem to be the most conspicuous lady-artist who has taken up the designing of artistic posters in the States. Her efforts date only from last February, when she did an advertisement for the " Boston Sunday Herald." Since then she has produced several designs which are held in considerable esteem by American collectors. Amongst other artists who have taken part in the poster movement on the other side of the Atlantic are the following : Messrs. Alder (" New York World," March 17th, 1895), Allen, Palmer Cox

("New Brownie Book"), C. Miles Gardner
("Boston Sunday Herald," February 10th,
1895, and March 10th, 1895), Oliver Her-
ford, Charles M. Howard ("Boston Sunday
Herald," April 21st, 1895), Frank King
("New York World," April 7th, 1895), H.
McCarter (the Green Tree Library), Moores
("St. Nicholas," November, 1894), Julius
A. Schweinfurth (Boston Festival Orchestra,
1895), W. Granville Smith ("Scribner's
Magazine," Christmas, 1894), W. L. Taylor,
Abby E. Underwood, R. Wills Irving, C.
H. Woodbury, Charles Hubbard Wright,
and William M. Paxton. The last named
has been chiefly associated with the "Boston
Sunday Herald," and for that journal he
has produced several posters of distinction.

My review of the artistic poster movement in America has been of necessity brief,
and cannot, therefore, be free from sins of
omission. In writing it, I have, where my
own knowledge has seemed to me insuffi-
cient, made use of the descriptive catalogue
of the collection of American posters published last May by Mr. Charles Knowles
Bolton, of Brookline, Massachusetts. From
the useful bibliography printed at the end
of this pamphlet, it would seem that the
movement has been watched from the first by
the American press with keen interest. So
far back as the year 1892, we find Mr.
Brander Matthews discussing the pictorial
poster in the "Century" magazine. In the

SCRIBNER'S

THE LAST QUARTER
CENTURY IN AMERICA

DESIGN BY KENYON COX

present year the subject has been dealt with
by writers in such important newspapers as

DESIGN BY SCOTSON CLARK.

the "New York Tribune" and the "Boston
Herald," to say nothing of such journals as

Y

" Scribner's Magazine," the " Critic," the
"Art Interchange," and the " Art Amateur."
Quite recently the English public have had
opportunities of seeing the best work by
French and native artists. It is to be hoped
that at the next poster exhibition they will
be afforded a chance of seeing what excellent
work American designers are doing in this
very practical branch of applied art.

A poster by Mr. E. A. Abbey, illustrated
on page 315, arrived too late for consideration in its proper place. It is entirely
worthy the great reputation of the artist
who has so kindly permitted us to reproduce
it here. The figure is in red scale armour,
bearing a shield with a red cross.

Christmas Number.

PRICE 25 cts
$3.00 Per Year.

ST. NICHOLAS.

DESIGN BY FRANCIS DAY.

THE
GREEN
TREE
LIBRARY

FOR SALE HERE

PUBLISHED BY
STONE & KIMBALL

DESIGN BY H. McCARTER.

CHAPTER X.

THE PICTORIAL POSTER IN COUNTRIES NOT ALREADY DISCUSSED.

THAT the picture poster was an incident of the ancient civilizations of China and Japan goes without saying. The scope, however, of this book does not embrace the Far East; the illustrated placard in the Orient would, indeed, be a subject in itself. In the matter of applied art it is difficult to conceive anything which the Chinese and the Japanese have not attempted. They seem, from the earliest days, to have been consumed with a passion for decoration; nothing which by any chance admitted of ornament was left undecorated. It behoves the societies which are formed for the purpose of illustrating the artistic antiquities of these wonderful countries to concern themselves with the dawn and history of the pictorial poster in the East. Certain it is that the illustrated advertisement abounded, as it abounds to-day, in the cities of both the nations now being discussed. It is, indeed, found in the less advanced civilization of Burma, and of

the various principalities which form our
Indian Empire.   To pass from Asia to Spain
is to travel a long way.   In Spain, at the
present moment, the illustrated placard is
receiving no small attention at the hands
of artists who, however discouraged and
ill-paid, are determined to do all that in
them lies to raise the country which produced
Murillo to the position she once held among
art-producing nations.   A recent writer in
the "Sketch" grows enthusiastic over the
Spanish *affiche*.   "Spanish posters," he tells
us, "are a delight.   Well drawn, vividly but
truly coloured, and perfectly printed, they
shine down from walls and hoardings, attracting all passers-by.   They depict the glories of
coming fairs and bull-fights, and are couched
in terms calculated to draw money from a
stone.   The announcement that a famous
matador will kill, or assist to kill, *Seis
Escogidos Toros*, throws the Spanish reader
into a state of frenzy.   Not infrequently
some incident is depicted with frank realism.
A bull standing over a dead horse gives an
opportunity to the artist to draw the unfor-
tunate horse disembowelled and lying on
blood-stained sand, while the bull's hide
shows the marks of the lance-thrusts, and
his horns are likewise stained with blood.
Colour-printing is so good in these regions of
perpetual sunlight that nearly every detail
of a matador's costume can be given.   The
poster artists are splendid when they depict

POSTER DESIGNED TO ADVERTISE AN ENTERTAINMENT AT
SEVILLE.

SPANISH POSTER FOR A BULL-FIGHT.

POSTER DESIGNED TO ADVERTISE AN ENTERTAINMENT AT
SEVILLE.

SPANISH POSTER FOR A FAIR.

DESIGN BY JOSEPH SATTLER.

Z

movement ; they are satisfactory in their
purely decorative work, but figures in repose
are apt to become 'woodeny.' In point of
colour, Spain beats France ; and as France
is so much in advance of England, it
scarcely needs a Euclid to demonstrate that
English posters cannot be compared to those
of Spain. The latter exhibit at times an
admirable sense of distance and proportion,
which serves to show that their designers
learnt to draw before they began to paint."
The four examples reproduced here will
serve to indicate the type of Spanish poster
most frequently met with. Whether Spain,
in the matter of the pictorial placard, is in
advance of France or not, is a question of
taste. However brilliant the colour of the
Spanish *affiche*, the design seems to me to
lack boldness. Take, for example, the
"Gran Feria de Cordoba, 1895 ;" in this
case the whole thing appears to be a series of
elaborate details rather than a bold and
impressive design. The poster in Spain,
however, is rapidly becoming of interest,
dealing as it does with fascinating and
essentially picturesque subjects. It is difficult to obtain exact information concerning
the artists who design posters in Spain ; the
examples which I reproduce here, I cannot
attribute to anybody with any degree of
certainty.

The Teutonic temperament is in no sense
akin to the Spanish, and the pictorial posters

of Germany are utterly unlike those of Spain.
For the most part the Germans have, in the
past, been addicted to elaborate and often
admirably-executed lithographs, such, for
instance, as that done by Ernest Klint for the
Musical and Theatrical Exhibition held at
Vienna in 1892. A new movement is, it
appears, making itself conspicuous just now.
The younger generation of German designers
seem to be as anxious to experiment in the
making of posters as those of France and
England. Joseph Sattler, a designer of
considerable originality and great dexterity,
who has studied Albrecht Dürer with great
advantage to his own work, has designed a
very curious little window bill to advertise
"Pan." It is reproduced here, and its strange
individuality, its ingenuity, will not fail to
make an impression upon those who look at
it closely. The lettering is devised in an
extraordinary way, and Sattler may be
congratulated on the results of an interesting
experiment. Very different to the work of
Sattler is that of Franz Stück. This represents a classical head in mosaic, and
advertises an exhibition of the Munich
Secessionists, a body of experimental
painters and designers of rapidly-growing
importance. The tendency of the illustrated
poster in Austria is much the same as it is in
Germany. Some admirable bills have been
designed in Italy. Of its particular kind, I
have seen few things better than a large and

DESIGN BY FRANZ STÜCK.

DESIGN BY EVENEPOEL.

DESIGN BY DUYCK.

La Libre Esthétique
MUSÉE MODERNE
tous les jours de 10 à 5 heures.
SALON ANNUEL
ARTS GRAPHIQUES - ARTS PLASTIQUES
OUVERTURE SAMEDI 23 FÉVRIER
prix d'entrée 1 franc, le dimanche 50 cent.
le jour de l'ouverture 5 fr, carte permanente 10 fr.
CONCERTS - CONFÉRENCES.
SEDGWICK

DESIGN FOR THE "LIBRE ESTHETIQUE."

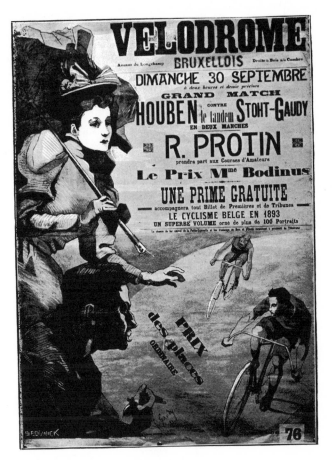

DESIGN BY GAUDY.

sombre poster to advertise Verdi's " Otello."
At the same time, the Italian posters are not
of a very distinctive type, nor does Italian
taste concerning them appear to be very
fastidious. The crude, enormous, and vulgar
advertisements for Buffalo Bill's exhibition
created quite a sensation in Rome when that
redoubtable personage deigned to visit the
most august of European capitals. The
modern Romans forgot their Michael Angelo
in the ecstasy induced by the latest enormity
of the American colour printer. It may be
noted that some of the posters done for the
Italian railway companies are bright and gay
as an Italian summer itself. The pictorial
poster would not seem to have taken a great
hold on Russia, nor, judging from a comparatively recent visit, has it made much headway
in Scandinavia. In Holland, the present
artistic vitality and enterprise of which are at
once so astonishing and gratifying, one meets
with very few posters of conspicuous merit.
In Belgium, on the other hand, there are signs
that the poster movement has affected not a
few artists of distinction. The placard by
Evenepoel, designed to advertise a publication in connection with the Antwerp
Exhibition, is excellent in colour and pattern
and most decidedly original, owing very little
to any foreign examples. Duyck's "Cortège
des Fleurs (Ville de Bruxelles)" is decorative
and pleasing. This artist has also designed
another placard to advertise Spa (Ferme de

Frahinfaz).   To Delville we owe a curious
little placard, in the Symbolist manner,
which advertised " Pour l'art, Ier exposition
à Bruxelles;" the advertisement for the second
exhibition was the work of Ottevaere.   A
fantastic and rather picturesque poster was
done to announce one of the annual exhibitions of "La Libre Esthetique." It represents
a strange-looking human being standing
among flowers, under a lurid sky, and holding in his hands a decorative scroll, upon
which the legend is inscribed.   Amongst
other interesting Belgian placards are the
"Velodrome Bruxellois" by G. Gaudy, the
"Paul Hankar" by A. Crespin, and a poster
in monochrome in imitation of a bas-relief
bearing the legend "La plus noble force
sociale est le Droit."   All of these are reproduced here.   It may be noted in conclusion that most of the Belgian posters
show strong signs of French influence.

DESIGN BY X. M.

A A

DESIGN BY A. CRESPIN.

DESIGN BY LEON BARDENNE.

CHAPTER XI.

THE PRICE OF THE PICTORIAL POSTER; AND CONCLUDING NOTE.

IT is obviously impossible to state accurately the price of the artistic poster, insomuch as fluctuations take place almost daily, and, moreover, the numerous dealers vary in their quotations in an extraordinary degree. Under these circumstances, the present chapter is written as a matter of current record, rather than with the idea that it will be of any permanent value for purposes of reference. It may be stated at the outset, that in dealing with the value of the poster, rarity has in the first place to be taken into consideration; and thus it happens that, while delightfully artistic designs are comparatively inexpensive, posters which are quite unattractive from the point of view of art are often very costly. The prices which follow are for the most part taken from the catalogues of M. Edmond Sagot of Paris, and Mr. Bella of London, the latter of whom, by the organization of exhibitions and in other ways, has rendered material assistance to English collectors. In fact, to some extent, he has called the English collector into existence.

As an example of the price of the poster of which the interest is archæological rather than artistic, one may instance a placard, dated the 20th of February, 1649, which deals with the opening and closing of the gates of Paris. Its only claim to be considered pictorial consists in the fact that it is ornamented with a woodcut representing the arms of the city. Many similar productions were executed in relation to London and to other English towns. The price asked for it three or four years ago was thirty francs. Interesting from another point of view are the illustrated posters which have heralded new books, or new editions of books, by great writers. Three of these, relating to the works of Balzac, and including one with woodcuts by Meissonier and Tony Johannot, are valued at twelve francs.

It is time, however, to pass from pictorial posters, which are interesting on account of age or literary association, to those which derive their value from their qualities as works of art. In this class some of the highest prices are obtained by the French artists who, for the most part, were the contemporaries, or immediate successors, of Gavarni. The best posters of this master are extremely difficult to procure, and examples in a fine state realize large sums.

For the "Œuvres Choisis" bill, together with that designed to advertise an illustrated edition of Balzac's "Philosophie de la Vie Conjugale," something over a hundred francs is asked, while less important works can be obtained for five-and-twenty or thirty francs. It goes without saying that the smallest tear or other injury, however neatly and skilfully repaired, heavily discounts the value of works by Gavarni and the men of his time; but even slightly damaged examples are eagerly sought for, as it is almost impossible to obtain perfect ones. Of the productions of Edouard de Beaumont, two of the rarest are the "Nains Célèbres," already mentioned, and the "Diable Amoureux." For an exceptionally fine proof of the former, as much as a hundred francs has been asked, while the latter, which is very rare, commands about sixty francs. Sums scarcely less formidable are given for the better posters of Grandville, and fifty francs for a good Tony Johannot is not by any means an exceptional price, although unimportant specimens of his work may be picked up in Paris for a few sous. The excursions of Gustave Doré into the art of the poster were very few. His most important work was perhaps the "Légende du Juif Errant," a fine proof of which realizes sixty francs or more. Posters by Vivant Beaucé, Castelli, Cham, Victor

Coindre, Charles Devrits, H. Emy, A. Farcy, and others of the same period, for the most part command sums comparatively small; the best productions of Bertall, Calame, Monnier, and C. Nanteuil, on the other hand, are only a little less expensive than those of Gavarni and the more distinguished designers of his time.

Of posters by designers still living, those of Chéret have been most assiduously collected. It is probable that a complete set of his works does not exist; even one which is fairly representative, and includes some of his earlier and rarer *affiches*, is extremely valuable. In the Sagot catalogue of 1891, over five hundred and fifty posters by Chéret are described, and of these no less than eighty are priced at twenty francs or more. Since the publication of the catalogue, their value has steadily increased, and it is uncertain if many of them can now be procured at all. The collector of modest means need not, however, regret that the older and rarer examples of Chéret are beyond his reach, for the artist's more recent posters are the best that he has accomplished. For a comparatively small outlay, one may secure the flower of Chéret's work. Amongst the most valuable of his posters are two, of very large size, designed to advertise some Arabs who appeared with the Paris Hippodrome when it visited London in 1887. The price asked for

them is over two pounds.) They seem
to have escaped the attention of French
collectors from the fact that they were posted
exclusively in London.   The set of four

FOLIES - BERGERE

LaLoie Fuller

DESIGN BY CHÉRET.

Loie Fuller bills, in all of which the design
is the same but the colouring different, is
worth between thirty and forty shillings.
These designs are among the most daring

and characteristic specimens of Chéret's amazing colour, and as they only measure forty-nine by thirty-three inches, they are of manageable size, and should find their way into the portfolio of every collector. The set of unlettered decorative panels which were described in an earlier part of the book, is at present sold by all dealers for five pounds. It goes without saying that proofs before letters, or prints on special paper, of the posters of Chéret, or of nearly any other artist, are much more valuable than ordinary copies.

Most of the posters of other living French artists may still be procured for a few shillings, but it is extremely improbable that such a state of things will long continue to be the case. Already examples by men of the modern school, such as Toulouse - Lautrec, Anquetin, Bonnard, Steinlen, and Ibels, are in great demand, and collectors should use the present opportunity to procure a series of these curiously interesting designs before the prices rise. Even now, Lautrec's first attempt, "Le Pendu," has become *rarissime*, and is valued at something over a sovereign. What has happened in this case will doubtless happen in the case of " La Reine de Joie," " Jane Avril," and Lautrec's other posters. The designs of Grasset are rapidly taking their place by the side of those of Chéret in the estimation of collectors, with the result that several of them command large prices. Thus the " Librairie Romantique," which was offered in 1891 for three francs, was priced by the same dealer in November, 1894, at twenty. What is going on in the case of Chéret, Grasset, and Lautrec, is going on, though it may be somewhat less rapidly, in the case of those other artists who have assisted to make the French *affiche* the charming and artistic thing it is.

(The posters of those artists who were the pioneers of the artistic poster movement in England are extremely rare. They worked in the days before the English collector existed, and any copies of their designs not actually posted, probably fell into the hands of the waste-paper dealer. (I have been unable to trace any copies of the advertisement done by Fred Walker for " The Woman in White," but the original design has been recently exhibited in London, and the price put upon it by its owners is seventy guineas. (Copies of Mr. Walter Crane's " Hippodrome " bill are extremely rare, as are those designed by Professor Herkomer for the " Magazine of Art," " Black and White," and the exhibition of his own works. (Turning to the younger men, it is interesting to note that Mr. Dudley Hardy's " Yellow Girl " sells in Paris for twenty francs, the large " Gaiety Girl " for half as much, and the smaller bills for the same play for five francs.) The first poster which this artist did for "St. Paul's" is very difficult to meet with; it will doubtless be among the most valuable of Mr. Hardy's designs. Mr. Beardsley's "Avenue" poster is quoted neither by Mr. Bella nor M. Sagot, and it may therefore be concluded that it is almost impossible to obtain it. The other posters of this designer are steadily increasing in value, and are eagerly sought for by collectors on both sides of the Channel. Mr. Greiffenhagen's "Pall Mall" poster, which has met with much success abroad, is worth about half a sovereign. The dainty little bill which Mr. Wilson Steer did for the exhibition of his paintings at the Goupil Gallery fetches about the same amount, and is rapidly becoming scarce. It is pleasant to think that the early efforts of English artists are welcomed by French collectors as enthusiastically as the masterpieces of French artists by collectors in England.

The poster is obviously difficult to collect, because of its size. Not all of us are proprietors of such an immensity as the Chicago Exhibition. Most of us, on the other hand, could paper a room with posters of Lautrec alone. Everybody, however, can put the smaller bills into a portfolio, while the larger ones may be mounted as ordinary school maps. The collecting of pictorial posters needs nothing more than a little heroism.

*　　　*　　　*　　　*　　　*

In the foregoing chapters, I have attempted to outline the history of art as applied to the poster, and to give an account of the pictorial placard in the present state of its development. The number of names, eminent in the history of various modern arts and crafts, who have applied themselves to the production of the pictorial poster seems to me to justify the publication of this book. (The fact that men so highly endowed as Chéret and Lautrec deliberately choose to appeal to the public chiefly by means of the *affiche*, well knowing that their gallery is the common hoarding, places the illustrated poster outside the bounds of ridicule.) A modern art critic of high repute and of enormous energy has assured us that, in these days, to neglect the poster is mere folly on the part of those who care for the application of taste and skill to the objects of everyday life. We are apt to talk of artistic periods ; periods when the most ordinary objects had an æsthetic character of their own. It seems to me to be full of promise for the future that the hoarding should be among the first necessities of modern civilization to be rendered charming by the skill and imagination of the artist. Art is generally supposed to be inimical to commerce, and commerce inimical to art, yet here we have the two combining to the advantage of both, and succeeding in making the beautiful an incident of the necessary.

CHISWICK PRESS :—CHARLES WHITTINGHAM AND CO
TOOKS COURT, CHANCERY LANE, LONDON.